LINDA HART-HEWINS / NANCI GOLDMAN / FRAN PARKIN

INTEGRATED PROGRAMS FOR ADOLESCENTS

Pembroke Publishers Limited

To the students who have inspired us.

©1993 Pembroke Publishers
538 Hood Road
Markham, Ontario L3R 3K9

Canadian Cataloguing in Publication Data

Hart-Hewins, Linda
  Integrated programs for adolescents

Includes bibliographical references and index.
ISBN 1-55138-009-9

1. Interdisciplinary approach in education.
2. Mainstreaming in education. I. Goldman, Nanci.
II. Parkin, Fran. III. Title.

1B1628.H37 1993   370.'1   C93-094775-8

Editor: Joanne Close
Design: John Zehethofer
Cover Illustration: Julian Mulock
Typesetting: Jay Tee Graphics Ltd.

This book was produced with the generous assistance of the government of Ontario through the Ministry of Culture and Communications.

Printed and bound in Canada
9 8 7 6 5 4 3 2 1

Contents

Acknowledgements

This book is the outcome of our collaboration with dedicated educators who have shared their expertise and thoughtful reflections on classroom practice.

We are indebted to the staff of Bloor Collegiate for their assistance in providing course materials and especially to Moira Wong, Hawley Shields, Steve Bibla, Danny Di Felice and Dave Robinson for sharing with us their efforts to integrate curriculum.

A grateful thank you as well to the staff of Alexander Muir/Gladstone Public School for field-testing some of our thematic units.

Thanks to Bruce Singleton and Zig Parkin for their helpful suggestions for the science-fiction unit.

We would also like to acknowledge the influence of the work that Jim Cummins has done in advocating equitable programs for minority students.

Finally, we thank our families, Issie, Tamara, Elisa, Charlie, Zig, Stephanie and Christopher, who have supported us throughout the writing of this book.

Introduction

We are living in an exciting world that is changing at an unprecedented rate. Some of the trends emerging from this evolvement — population growth and mobility, a global economy, evolving family structures, the increasing role of technology — have major implications for education. Today's students will need to acquire knowledge, skills and values that were unheard of in past generations in order to fulfil their role in the new century.

Changes in the educational system are happening at all levels. We have focused on one group, adolescent learners between the ages of twelve and fifteen, in an effort to provide strategies to help meet their diverse needs. Students of this age must see the relevance of what they are learning. They must be able to connect the enormous amounts of information available to their existing knowledge and experiences because it is only through seeing relationships and establishing connections that they are able to make sense of their world. They need to connect new learning to real life in order to see how this learning fits into a larger picture. If adolescents are not afforded this opportunity, there is a danger that they will drop out of school and abdicate from academic learning. Teachers face an enormous challenge as they seek to support their students and make classroom learning relevant and worthwhile for all students.

It is the intention of this book to explore, in a practical manner, the ways in which teachers can create conditions that will successfully support young adolescent learners. We believe that a curriculum that provides integrated thematic units of work which encompass the learning of different subject disciplines will provide the framework from which students can see meaning and make vital connections among the learning of the classroom, their lives and the larger world.

We have organized this book in the following manner:

Chapter One: Getting to Know Our Students
- how students are different
- how students are the same

Chapter Two: Keys to the Future — Setting the Stage
- knowledge, skills and values that employers require
- reflections on teaching practices
- conditions that facilitate learning
- what students say about their school experiences
- what students say is important for them at school
- existing structures that impede the development of successful school environments and curricula

Chapter Three: Our Recipe for Success — Integrated Thematic Units of Study
- rationale for themes
- benefits for adolescent learners
- timetabling issues that are addressed by themes

Chapter Four: What You Need Is a Plan — Begin with Your Subject Area
- criteria for a good theme
- phases of a theme: planning, immersion, response, wrap-up
- theme ingredients: whole-group activities, Learners' Circle, response activities, assessment and evaluation criteria
- format of a theme: focused study, core study
- direction of a theme
- order themes may take throughout the year
- suggested yearly plan

Chapter Five: Try This! One Way to Begin
- science fiction, a focused-study theme: rationale, intended learning outcomes, whole-group, small-group and independent activities, timeline, sample evaluation guides, bibliography*
- ecology, a core-study theme: rationale, intended learning outcomes, whole-group, small-group and independent activities, timeline, sample evaluation guides, bibliography*
- additional strategies for setting context
- sample games

Chapter Six: Still Not Satisfied?

- frustrations experienced when integration with other subject disciplines hasn't occurred
- hazardous waste, a core-study theme: rationale, intended and common learning outcomes, whole-group, small-group and independent activities, evaluation criteria, bibliography*
- survival, a focused-study theme: whole-group, small-group and independent activities, bibliography*, evaluation suggestions

Chapter Seven: Almost There!

- frustrations with theme use
- advice when beginning integrated thematic units of study
- immigration, a focused-study theme: common learning outcomes, timeline, whole-group, small-group and independent activities, bibliography*, evaluation method
- social and racial justice, a core-study theme: whole-group, small group, and independent activities, bibliography*

---

* Bibliographies for each study unit are featured on pages 84-92.

CHAPTER ONE

Getting to Know Our Students

Our classrooms contain students who vary in their abilities, their desire to learn and the way they show their thinking. Some prefer to demonstrate their learning through reading and writing activities while others are more comfortable listening and making oral presentations. Still others prefer to view, build and create to show their learning. All students must be given equal opportunities to demonstrate their understandings, thinking and problem-solving abilities in varied ways for society needs many kinds of learners to face future challenges. Causes for differing learning abilities vary — school interruptions, learning styles and abilities, and social and emotional upheavals are some of the possible contributors. In the past, many students were excluded from mainstream classrooms; however, educators and parents now understand the benefits of including all students in one educational setting with an open-ended curriculum and appropriate in-class support.

Our students represent a range of cultural and linguistic backgrounds that reflect the mobility of the world's population. Students of many nationalities work side-by-side, each with their set of cultural values, customs and beliefs. For many students, the language of instruction is not their first language. In most urban classrooms, students have varying degrees of proficiency in English. Some, although conversationally proficient, have not acquired the necessary skills in English to understand text, provide information orally and offer written responses using conventional forms of grammar, spelling, punctuation and form. Others are fully literate in two or more languages while some students speak only the language of instruction.

In the past, those students who did not speak the language of instruction well enough to keep up with the academic work of the classroom were segregated — the learning of a new language was isolated from the learning of the content areas. Increasingly, however, educators have looked to research that suggests this practice is not only counterproductive to learning a new language and curriculum content but also lowers learners' self-esteem. We now know that language is best learned in the company of more sophisticated language users, for it is often the social interaction with more fluent classmates that provides the need and purpose for the learner to take the risks necessary to acquire the new language.

There are two types of language proficiency — conversational and academic. Conversational proficiency means that students can converse in the new language to interact with their peers to make their needs understood. Jim Cummins, in his book *Empowering Minority Students* (1989), notes that it takes approximately two years of exposure to English for conversational skills to approach native-like levels. Academic proficiency, the ability to use language to think and learn, to comprehend academic material and to understand oral and written instructions without the benefit of contextual cues such as gestures and illustrations, takes five years or more.

In past years, we thought that speaking and writing in one's first language while learning English was harmful. Classroom teachers discouraged students from conversing in languages other than English because it was assumed that the student would become confused. The opposite, it seems, is true; once a student understands a concept, it is much easier to transfer this understanding to another language. Students who come to our country with a firm foundation in their first language are able to learn a new language faster than their non-literate counterparts.

As teachers, we know how important pride is to classroom performance. If students are valued at school, they will take risks to learn. If their language is not valued and their culture, as a consequence, not reflected, students will probably resist learning. It is important, then, to include all students and their cultures in the curriculum. In our classes, we include books in first language to reflect the classroom population and to help students in their conceptual understanding of themes. We also provide tutoring for students in their first language if they are not literate. As you read the theme outlines in later chapters, you'll notice that we suggest providing books in first language for some students.

Students arriving from other countries are in more vulnerable positions than second-language learners of past generations. Cummins (1989) reports that immigrants who have lived for many years under regimes of oppression continue to find themselves in disadvantaged situations in their new country. As well, those who emigrate to centers where there is no strong host community are least likely to assimilate successfully. They have little in the way of options except school because, unlike immigrants of the past, there are few jobs available for unskilled workers who do not speak the local language.

Teachers today, then, face enormous challenges if they are to meet the academic and social needs of such a diverse student population. All students need to be valued and must be viewed as rich classroom resources, vital to making the work of the classroom relevant and purposeful. Although they have varying abilities, hold differing attitudes toward learning and represent a variety of cultural, linguistic and economic backgrounds, students have much in common.

Transitions occur in all parts of their lives. Young adolescents continuously negotiate who and what they are, vacillating between independence and dependence, between confidence and insecurity, between being outgoing and withdrawn. They struggle with the establishment of personal sets of values, looking for commonalities and compromises between home and peers. Relationships with the latter occupy much of their time and their influence is paramount. Many are concerned with issues of sexuality. Relationships with family members may be strained, as adolescents are often self-centered, quick to question and may only engage in activities that interest them. They seek relevance in their lives and want to know what the school curriculum has to do with them. If they see no meaning, they are quick to say ''no.''

These are our students. From diverse backgrounds, they share similar needs, interests and characteristics. They live in a rapidly changing world, a world that is driven by sophisticated technology, enormous population growth, diminishing resources and growing tensions between those groups who hold power, influence and wealth and those who do not. What are the knowledge, skills and values that these students will need in the future?

CHAPTER TWO

Keys to the Future — Setting the Stage

The world these students will enter on leaving school differs greatly from that faced by previous generations. To help them prepare for this world, students must become:

- self-activated learners who accept responsibility for shaping and defining their learning and actions;
- creative problem-solvers who think of questions and find new answers to old problems;
- critical thinkers who question information, attitudes, practices;
- life-long learners who continue to undertake new training, skills, knowledge and attitudes throughout their lives;
- holistic learners who can absorb, reflect upon, analyze and synthesize information, looking for relevant connections within the larger picture;
- independent learners who seek out connections between known learning and new learning;
- co-operative learners who can work as a team to solve problems;
- empathetic members of a cosmopolitan workforce who understand and appreciate various points of view and who are open to learning about other cultures;
- bilingual members of the community.

These are only some of the characteristics that students will need in order to be secure, fulfilled citizens. If schools are to serve students well, it is obvious that we must rethink what we view as learning. No longer will it be sufficient for students to regurgitate a set of facts for a two-hour exam; to offer pre-determined answers to pre-determined teacher-composed questions; to work in isolation; to accept all teachings without question; or to view customs, beliefs and practices that are different from their own as aberrant. To enable our students to live and work in a diverse but inclusive society, we must help them to become self-motivated, independent, creative, reflective and critical questioners who take responsibility for their learning and actions.

It is imperative that teachers determine their students' backgrounds and needs, and the knowledge, skills and values that they will require to have control over their future. Teachers need to reflect on these understandings as they plan for learning environments that are conducive to the shared needs, interests and characteristics of such a diverse adolescent population.

Conditions for Learning

There are a number of conditions that need to be in place before we can expect students to thrive in their school environment. Among recent research in the area of education, Brian Cambourne's work is helpful in determining essential elements of conducive learning environments. His work offers insights into what environments in our schools and classrooms should look like if all students are to see relevance in their learning, form bonds of trust with teachers and gain the knowledge, skills and values necessary for adult life.

Cambourne's beliefs about learning are based on his studies of how young children learn to talk. His extensive work in this area has led him to conclude that there are seven conditions that facilitate learning; if teachers program, plan and timetable for these conditions, learning environments that facilitate true learning can be constructed.

Teachers naturally create most of these conditions for optimum learning environments in their classrooms. They plan and timetable for necessary components of immersion, use and demonstration. They recognize, honor and encourage approximations, both verbal and written, and are careful to offer positive and appropriate responses to students' learning. Teachers' words and actions show that they expect students to learn. What often presents a challenge for teachers, however, is setting up learning environments that allow and encourage today's diverse students to take responsibility for their learning. Without this inner commitment, there is no engagement and as a consequence, no real learning.

Seven Conditions to Facilitate Learning

1. Learners must be immersed in learning.
2. They must be exposed to numerous demonstrations of learning by more experienced learners.
3. They must have ample opportunity to practise and use this new learning in authentic and real situations where they are surrounded by more experienced learners and teachers whom they like and trust.
4. More experienced learners and teachers must expect learners to learn.
5. They must offer positive responses to learners' attempts at learning.
6. They must accept learners' approximations of learning as valid.
7. True learning will not occur unless learners accept responsibility for their learning. They must reach out and say, "I can do that, I want to do that, I will question and risk possible failure but I will continue and I will succeed."

Our failure to set the stage for the seventh condition is borne out by results of one country-wide survey. High school dropouts and graduates were asked to reply to the question, "How could school have been made better for you?"

Here is a sample of their responses.

"I never could see meaning in what we had to do. I wish we had studied things I wanted to learn about."

"It made no sense to me."

"I wasn't interested in what we had to do. I didn't see any need to learn all that stuff."

"It was so boring but I did it because the teacher told me to."

"I did what I had to, to get through. I wanted to be a teacher and I needed my high school diploma to go on to university."

Obviously, for a number of students, many of the knowledge, skills and values that they were expected to acquire had little relevance. Despite teachers' efforts to provide effective learning environments, many students refused to take responsibility for their learning and did not engage in the learning of the classroom.

Teachers need to answer some critical questions:

1. How can we make the work of our classrooms meaningful to the interests, needs and concerns of all students?
2. How do we help students to see a purpose for learning and take responsibility for it?
3. How can we integrate the essential need for each student to see the relevance of his or her learning with required learning outcomes dictated by local educational authorities?

Answers to some of these questions can be found in the responses one group of twelve- and thirteen-year-olds offered when asked the question, "What was the most important thing for you this year at school?"

"I liked the teacher because she cared about me and my work."

"I liked math. It's easy and I'll need it when I go to work."

"I liked social studies because I learned about all the places I could travel to."

"None of it had anything to do with me."

From these responses, it's clear that young adolescents, regardless of backgrounds and interests, want two things: a relevant and meaningful curriculum; and teachers whom they like and whom they perceive as being interested in them as individuals. We believe that more positive conditions can be created by educators if we rethink the manner in which we expect and allow learners and teachers to negotiate a satisfactory curriculum for all.

School Structures Can Block Relevant Learning

At present, many teachers work in institutional frameworks that make it difficult to create the kinds of learning environments that students want and that are critical if learners are to be hooked on learning. Teachers, for the most part, work in isolation from their colleagues. Any co-operative planning and discussion that takes place usually happens within the confines of specific subject disciplines. These discussions typically result in conformity of learning experiences, rather than experiences of a diverse nature that will interest a range of students. For example, after extensive discussions by English teachers at a large metropolitan high school, it was agreed that all grade nine students would read *The Chrysalids,* "The Lottery" and "Trifles" from *15 American One-Act Plays* in the first term. This linear thinking dictates that all learners, regardless of interests and learning abilities, perform the same activities using the same materials at the same time. Such restrictions do not make for truly engaged learners who, in such a system, have few opportunities to see the reason, and hence the purpose, for learning. Many students are unable to read, comprehend and respond to the materials and, because they rarely help to plan and shape their learning, accept no ownership for it.

Collaboration among various subject disciplines may also be rare. Teacher discussions are often dominated by conflicts in timetabling, time constraints and the inadequacies of students, instead of issues such as identifying commonalities in programming and curriculum. As a result, students move from one learning experience to another with few, if any, connecting links. Schooling becomes a succession of discrete, pre-planned experiences that for many make little sense in terms of real life.

Because of the nature of timetables, teachers are obliged to deliver prescribed content-driven curriculum to a different group of students every forty to seventy-five minutes, on average. Scheduling learning into tiny, discrete, unconnected subject chunks makes it almost impossible for the student to become immersed in learning — lack of time and the tyranny of the bell become serious obstacles to the process. As well, the changing composition of each class makes it difficult for teachers and students to get to know one another as individuals with specific interests, needs and experiences. Bonds of trust and understanding between students and teachers, a condition that students have identified as important to their positive feelings toward school and learning, sprout only in defiance of these school environments.

Change Is Necessary

Obviously, this structure of teaching and learning must change if we are to heed the views of our students and put into place the conditions that facilitate learning. The orthodoxy of timetabling and the delivery of discrete subject disciplines by a variety of specialists must be challenged so that we can provide students with the opportunity to find relevance in their schooling and to come to know one or two adults with whom they can form a bond of trust. We know from our experiences as learners and teachers that we learn best when we:

18

- have some ownership of learning;
- see some need or relevance to learning;
- understand personal and global connections of learning;
- have time to be immersed in learning;
- feel we will be successful;
- feel secure in the learning environment;
- trust the teacher.

Teachers have the expertise and the creativity to change this structure of teaching and learning to one in which learning for all students is facilitated rather than thwarted.

In reshaping our thinking about more effective ways to program for twelve- to fifteen-year-olds, we looked at a number of successful models. We found that many of the structures already in place in the primary and junior grades of our school system offered some of the best solutions. The notion of having a team of teachers offer a group of mixed ability students an integrated curriculum based on broad themes of learning appealed to us. We knew that such a structure allows for an optimal learning environment to be created, for student ownership and relevance of learning to be established, for the time students require to be truly engaged in learning and for opportunities for students to form a bond with one or two significant adults.

CHAPTER THREE

Our Recipe for Success — Integrated Thematic Units

We recognized that through the deliberate creation of broad integrated units of study that encompass more than one subject discipline, we could replicate conditions similar to those already in place in many elementary classrooms. Not only would thematic units ease the transition from one learning environment to another, but they would also begin to help make our classroom learning more relevant and connected.

Why Broad Themes?

Broad-based integrated thematic units of study make it possible for learners to find paths for learning and to see the relevancy of their learning. By allowing learners to select areas of interest from a menu of sub-topics within a broad theme, teachers will see that students are more likely to find a topic of relevance and interest than if they are forced to study specifics of a narrow topic. By encouraging and facilitating student choice of the areas of interest to be pursued, teachers allow learners to take responsibility for their learning. Students' ownership over learning is an elusive condition that must be in place if true learning is to occur.

Prescribed Learning Becomes More Relevant

In selecting broad-based themes as the basis for learning, teachers have the opportunity to set prescribed learning outcomes mandated by local educational authorities into a wider, potentially more relevant context. For example, instead of spending hours in a history class asking students to focus on the Rebellion of 1837, think of how much more relevant this topic would be if it were embedded in the broader theme of global conflict. Teachers can help students understand the issues of the Rebellion in the context of present life. Students' personal experiences of war and reports in the news can be used to put prescribed curriculum into the relevant context of their lives and experiences.

Time to Become Immersed in Learning

We believe that the creation of thematic units of work can help relieve the constraints of an already crowded timetable. By timetabling the work of an English class with the work of one or more of the content areas, longer blocks of time can be found within a busy, often fragmented timetable. Similarly, timetabling the work of a science class with that of a mathematics class creates longer blocks of time. Students and teachers no longer have to refocus their thinking on new and discrete subject disciplines. With subject integration housed in the framework of themes, they can now spend longer periods of time discussing, researching, questioning and thinking about specific interests within a broader context. The precious commodity of time is available for students to become engrossed in their work and to sustain their concentration long enough to see their efforts come to fruition.

Time for Building Bonds of Trust Between Learner and Teacher

Themes that span more than one subject discipline allow more flexibility between learners and teachers. When the framework of integrated themes is used, students have one teacher instead of a different teacher for each subject discipline incorporated into the theme. For example, if history and English teachers combined their learning outcomes and time to offer a common theme on conflict, then the students have one teacher, not two. Conditions are put in place whereby the critical bond of trust and caring between learner and teacher can be forged. In many traditional non-semestered schools, teachers instruct, on average, six groups of students per day. By using an integrated thematic approach, teachers might only interact with three groups of students in a day — one group in the morning for a double period, another group split before and after the lunch hour for a double period, and the final group in the afternoon. Instead of following the timetable structure in a traditional setting, each group of students remains constant, moving together as a group. This allows time to trust, to learn about each other as learners and to feel secure in the environment. School becomes a more personal place.

Success for a Diverse Student Population

We believe that broad units of work organized around a theme or issue allow the teacher flexibility to vary the forms of instruction, materials and responses that are necessary if all learners are to be successful. Teacher-delivered lectures are replaced with whole-class, small-group and individual work. Students work in co-operative groupings where they are both learners and teachers. The teacher becomes one of many resources that help students find answers to their questions.

The single textbook that many students in the past were unable to read is now replaced by a variety of resources — magazines, picture books, newspapers, novels, brochures, pamphlets, charts or films that offer students a variety of information about their topic of interest. By timetabling the activities of an English, art and drama class with the knowledge, skills and values of a history or geography class, teachers give students opportunities to show their learning in a variety of ways. There is a purpose and context for oral presentations, debates, role playing, artistic impressions, construction and writing. By allowing students to select and vary the manner in which they display their learning and understanding, we provide for equity in our classrooms. Because we provide an environment in which all learners and their learning are valued, students feel secure and are more willing to risk future learning. Thematic units provide an enriched curriculum so that all students, whether gifted, learners of another language or learners who have been designated as challenged can experience, reflect upon and apply the knowledge, skills and values inherent in the units of study.

Sound like a good idea? Thematic units that span more than one subject appear to be an effective way to hook students on learning and provide for that elusive condition that promotes learners' responsibility for learning. Thematic units also provide the necessary time for students to become immersed in the learning, to feel secure in the environment and to trust and like the teacher. One question remains — where to begin?

CHAPTER FOUR

What You Need Is a Plan — Begin with Your Subject Area

Subject teachers must first examine the manner in which they deliver the content of their curriculum. Lecture-style instruction on a narrow, prescribed set of knowledge, skills and values no longer meets the needs of our diverse student population. The use of a textbook sets some learners up to fail while the traditional written test, exam or oral presentation allows only those students who are proficient in language skills to show their understanding. Units organized around a narrow focus that learners perceive as having no relevance to their lives may result in their disengagement from classroom learning. Broad-based themes centered on learning outcomes of an individual subject discipline allow for personal interest, offer a variety of resources, appeal to different learning styles and boost self-esteem, all factors that help to meet the needs of our students.

Choosing a Theme

Choosing an effective theme is crucial to the success of an integrated unit. Its content must be of interest to the students and have a direct correlation to their lives. It is our experience that successful themes:

- allow each student to find an area of interest;
- allow prescribed learning outcomes to be realized;
- have substance and relevance to the real world;
- are meaningful and age-appropriate;
- have a range of readily available resource materials;
- intrigue students once they are immersed;
- answer students' questions and concerns.

Themes such as beliefs/customs/cultures, relationships, the future, and social and racial justice and change offer students the scope to find reasons and paths for learning. Narrow themes such as mice, magnets and trees do not!

Structure

We have found that all themes, despite differing foci, timelines and format, have four phases: planning, immersion, response and wrap-up.

Planning

In this initial phase, we consult the guidelines prescribed by educational authorities, determine learning outcomes, consult with colleagues, gather resources and plan open-ended activities that will offer all students opportunities to show their learning.

Immersion

During this time, we raise the students' awareness of the topic — their time is spent discussing the topic in whole and small groups and in reading. We plan whole-group, small-group and independent activities for students to explore during this phase and the response and wrap-up phases that follow.

Response

As the title of this phase suggests, students spend time carrying out response activities designed to deepen their understanding of the issues and fulfil designated learning outcomes.

Wrap-up

Students work independently or in small groups to apply understanding of the area of interest they chose to explore.

Elements of Integrated Theme Units

WHOLE-GROUP ACTIVITIES

An important feature of thematic work is the time we spend each day with the class as a whole. During this time, we may read from a novel, short story or picture book, view a film, listen to a speaker or provide background information on the theme. We also take this opportunity as a large group to discuss issues, role play aspects of underlying issues of the theme, review strategies with which we want the students to become more familiar and teach new skills and knowledge.

LEARNERS' CIRCLES

Another important feature of thematic work that we do on a daily basis is the Learners' Circle, or Readers' Circle as it is known to some. This is a place where students come together in small groups to share their learning. Its focus will change from one subject to another. For example, in an English class students will share their reading and responses. In a science or mathematics class, the students and teacher may collectively solve problems, test hypotheses and look for patterns. In a history class, students may learn how to make a timeline of relevant historical events, relate issues of today to the facts of the past and research cause-and-effect relationships. Whatever its focus, this small-group time in the Learners' Circle is one of the critical underpinnings of successful theme work. Students of all abilities take part in the Learners' Circle — they are grouped heterogeneously so they can learn from one another.

The role of the teacher is critical during these small-group sessions. We

- facilitate the discussion, ensuring that all students have an opportunity to take part;
- use this time to observe and plan future teaching;
- carry out diagnostic and formative evaluations (keep a notebook handy to record observations systematically);
- demonstrate new strategies for response;
- plan time for the students to share their responses;
- help the students develop and use self- and peer-evaluation techniques.

Each day the teacher meets with a different Learners' Circle. During this time, the rest of the class is engaged in a series of independent, pair and small-group activities, which are divided into musts and choices. It is the students' responsibility to order and complete these tasks. When the teacher has finished with the Learners' Circle, there is an opportunity for interaction with those students who are working independently at assigned tasks or tasks of their own choosing.

Snapshot of Learners' Circle Time

Remaining students work at these
assigned tasks in order of their choice.

          / | \

Teacher meets   response   read   response —
with a different journal   and log   literary
Learners' Circle   reading   sociogram
each day for
15-20 minutes
and then circu-
lates among the
rest of the class.

OR

Remaining students work at these
assigned tasks in the order of their
choice or your request.

          / | \

Teacher meets   science   research   graph work
with a different experiment
Learners' Circle
each day for
15-20 minutes
and then circu-
lates among the
rest of the class.

Sample Timetables

75-minute time block

15 minutes	teacher reads to the whole class
15 minutes	teacher teaches a new response to the whole class — e.g., a literary sociogram
45 minutes	individual, pair or group work — teacher conferences with students who have signed up for a conference OR the teacher meets with a different Learners' Circle each day as the rest of the class works independently

OR

45 minutes	show a film, hear a speaker, etc.
30 minutes	debrief

OR

15 minutes	teacher reads to the whole class
45 minutes	teacher meets with one Learners' Circle while the rest of the class works independently at assigned activities
15 minutes	sharing

— — — — — — — — — — — — — — — — — — —

45-minute time block

15 minutes	teacher reads to the whole class
30 minutes	teacher teaches a new skill/knowledge to the whole class

OR

15 minutes	teacher reads to the whole class
30 minutes	teacher meets with one Learners' Circle while the rest of the class works independently at assigned activities

OR

45 minutes	Readers' Workshop

OR

45 minutes	Writers' Workshop

Response Activities

Response activities afford students ways of further creating meaning for themselves from gathered information. Students provided with opportunities to respond in a variety of ways benefit because they can select activities according to their abilities and interests, as well as display their understanding through a variety of demonstrations. These activities connect with other content areas since they highlight thinking skills common to all curriculum. The following responses help students personalize information and display understanding. Many of these ideas are not new, and there is a host of other strategies being tried by teachers and students all the time. Books such as *Literacy through Literature* by Terry Johnson and Daphne Louis and *Creating Classrooms for Authors* by Jerome Harste and Kathy Short contain wonderful ideas. We describe other activities later in the book in the context of specific theme work.

RESPONSE JOURNALS

Response journals are vehicles that can be used by teachers to encourage students to respond in a systematic way to their learning. They offer students an opportunity to find their voice and gain personal meaning from their learning. Students have a forum to state their opinions, link past and present learning and reflect on their feelings. In these journals, students can respond to materials they have read, stories they have shared, films they have viewed, speakers they have heard, discussions in which they participated and trips they have taken. Journals can take many forms; however, we prefer a letter form, complete with date, salutation and signature. Students write these letters to their teacher and, in some cases, to their peers. They have a quick response from the reader that further extends learning. Journals are a powerful vehicle to help students and teachers communicate about learning over time. The example on the next page is one grade seven student's response to the novel *Of Mice and Men*.

BUBBLE THINKING, CHARACTER PROFILE AND LITERARY SOCIOGRAMS

These activities help students to process the content of themes by depicting aspects and characters from reading materials, offering students an opportunity to express their understanding in pictorial form.

February 10, 1993.

Dear Mrs. Ramani,

The book I have read is called _Of Mice and Men_ by John Steinbeck.

A character who really stood out in my mind was Lennie, because he was mentally just like a little kid who didn't mean any harm. However, he also had super strength, and didn't know enough to control it. Because of his retardation he had been picked on. In some ways, he understood that he was a problem, and that he was causing George a lot of trouble. This was shown in one scene in which he was hiding by the river, waiting for George. He was obviously thinking of how he could stop being a nuisance to George. He expected George to bawl him out, and he said: "I'll go up into them hills and find a cave to live in!" However, he knew he couldn't survive without George. I thought Lennie was a very trusting, heart-warming character.

I think there are two principal messages in this book. The first is that everyone has dreams, but unfortunately, they don't necessarily come true. The second is the importance of friendship since loneliness makes us desperate.

I strongly recommend this book, because it's a beautiful story that has both humourous and sad aspects to it. It'll make you laugh and cry at the same time. I would recommend it to everyone who likes to hear a good story. Read it. You'll enjoy it!

Stephanie

Dear Stephanie,

I agree with you. It did make me laugh & cry. How important is it for people to have dreams? I'd be interested in your opinion.

Mrs. Ramani

29

Bubble Thinking
- Have students select four main scenes from their story.
- They fold a large piece of paper into four parts to represent the scenes. They draw the characters involved in each scene on one of the four parts.
- Students then add thought bubbles in which they write the thoughts of each character.
- With the students, discuss the differences and implications.

Character Profile
- Ask students to select a character from their reading or viewing.
- They draw, on a large piece of paper, a profile of the character.
- They then decide on words that describe the character's attributes and write them inside the profile.
- Students list physical descriptors of the character outside the drawing.

Literary Sociogram
- Have students use one of the selected resources and write the names of the main characters on a large piece of paper. They draw wide "pathways" between characters who have a relationship.
- Students fill in each pathway with words that describe the relationships between the characters.
- They note changes that might have occurred in these relationships.

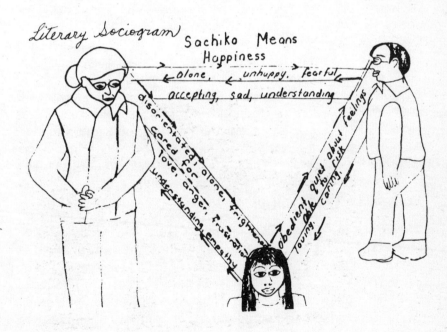

Retelling provides students with the opportunity to explore materials through oral and written work, art and dramatic creations. Have the students

- work in pairs or small groups and retell stories orally or in written form in English or in their first language by paraphrasing, elaborating and creating new endings;
- create a tableau (dramatic creation of a still-life scene of a story). The tableau can be silent and then brought to life on your signal;
- role play the part of the story to experience the feelings and speak through the voice of the characters in the story;
- visually re-create the story through art, construction, storyboard and video/filmstrip production.

Strategies for Assessment and Evaluation

Assessment is the reflection on learning for both teachers and students; evaluation, the interpretation for parents and students of the competencies that students demonstrate. Both assessment and evaluation must be ongoing in nature and take many forms if all learning is to be assessed and evaluated fairly. As teachers, we assess desired learning outcomes through a number of techniques that are mentioned in this text. Some of these strategies include observations of students' performances and analyses of collections of work and contributions in group and student-teacher conference settings. Throughout this book, we have included specific ways to help students reflect on their learning.

Format of the Theme

The format the theme follows depends largely on the availability of materials and time. We organize our thematic units in two distinct formats depending on materials, time and groupings of students. The first format — a focused study — is broad-based and has each student reading a different book or resource material. All resources have the same literary or content focus. Literary themes include science fiction, humor, myths and legends, and adventure; self and society themes include conflict, relationships, alienation and immigration; science themes include the environment, physiological change and human life. Students are grouped hetereogeneously with each group meeting once a week with the teacher in the Learners' Circle to discuss the content and ideas found in their materials, share their responses and findings and learn new ways of responding. This format usually takes longer than the second format, core study.

In core study, we work with a smaller number of resources on narrower topics such as pollution, Native people and early government. Students who are reading the same materials meet once a week with the teacher in the Learners' Circle to discuss ideas found in the materials and to share their responses.

The materials can be organized in a number of ways:

1. Select four or five books or texts. Choose materials for students that vary in reading proficiency and gather five or six copies of each. Ask the students to select the materials they wish to read. This forms natural groupings that will meet in the Learners' Circle to discuss the books they are reading. During the course of the theme, students are expected to read as many of these books as possible.
2. Select fifteen resources on the topic. Pair the students and have them work together on a response activity. Conference with each pair or group once a week.
3. Find a good resource and read it to the class. Have the students make collaborative responses in pairs or small groups. Conference with the groups or pairs. Plan time for whole-group reading, discussing and teaching new strategies.

Direction

The direction that each theme takes will depend on the interests and learning styles of the students. For example, one grade eight class explored the theme of social and racial justice. Within this theme, one group of students prepared a defense to present to the Supreme Court to argue for more severe charges for impaired drivers; a second group prepared a series of pictures and graphs to illustrate the manner in which the media depict the actions and lives of teenagers; a third group shared interviews they had conducted with family members who had lived in Europe during the Second World War; and a fourth group looked for bias by comparing several textbooks that offered an account of the "discovery" of North America by Christopher Columbus with recent articles on this event.

Order

The order in which individual themes are introduced depends on the students' interests, current events, available time and work of other teachers. We have found that it is not advisable, when beginning to implement thematic units of work, to plan more than one large unit of work each term. We intersperse our longer, more broad-based focused studies with the shorter and narrower core studies. The length of time each theme takes depends on the interest of the students, the depth to which the topic is examined and the availability of materials. Focused studies extend over a period of six to eight weeks while core studies take approximately three to four weeks of intensive work to complete.

A successful yearly plan for a history classroom may look something like this:

September core study	Contemporary Canada — students' points of view

October to mid-November
  focused study
	Life at the Turn of the
	Century
	— communities and
	  immigration patterns

Mid-November to mid- December core study	Social Inequality
January to mid-February focused study	Citizenship, Government and Law

Mid-February to mid-March
  core study
	World Economic Conflict
	— labor history, the
	  Depression

Mid-March to May focused study	Global Conflict — World Wars I and II
May to June core study	Post-War Changes and their Impact

CHAPTER FIVE

One Way to Begin — A Focused-Study Unit on Science Fiction

A colleague decided to explore this topic with his grade nine English class. "I was frustrated with using a single novel," he said. "Many of my students could not read it. I wanted to try a thematic approach in which I could make use of a range of reading materials. I wanted to give students some ownership over how they showed their understanding of the genre."

To begin, he selected science fiction. "I knew there was a good selection of reading materials available and that my students were interested in the topic," he reported. "The genre of science fiction provided me with the unique opportunity to have my students examine issues which face the individual, society and humanity from the perspective of the future." He used a focused-reading format because he knew there were available materials and the moral issues were broad enough for an indepth study.

He had some specific learning outcomes. He wanted his students to be able

- to identify and demonstrate an understanding of the elements of a successful science-fiction work;
- to create their own science-fiction work;
- to use this genre to demonstrate an awareness of some of the moral issues that face society;
- to demonstrate critical thinking skills;
- to present arguments that indicate a capacity to evaluate the merits of science-fiction text.

All work done during the eight weeks of the theme was related to these outcomes. They provided a focus for information collection, small- and large-group discussions and the content of the reading, writing, art, drama and media studies. The pages that follow detail his actions for each of the four phases.

Planning

Here are some of the steps he took in the planning stage.

1. He arranged to meet with the teacher-librarian to plan activities that would take place in the library. They decided that during the immersion phase the whole class would come to the library to hear a book talk on available materials; during the response stage, a group of students would work in the library each day under the supervision of the teacher-librarian. Thoughout these three weeks, students would work in pairs to identify a moral issue in their novels. They would research identified issues from a current perspective.

2. With the teacher-librarian's help, he compiled a large collection of science-fiction materials that were age-appropriate and represented a range of readability. He included Canadian and international works by both contemporary and classic authors so comparisons and contrasts in style and content could be made. He contacted local libraries and specialized bookstores for recommendations to pass on to his students, in addition to locating a number of appropriate films to view.

3. He contacted the Portuguese and Chinese Modern Languages teachers to obtain a selection of first-language materials because he had a number of students who were literate in their first language, but not in English. He realized if they were to take an active role in this study, their materials would have to be in first language.

4. He met with other teachers who taught these students and secured from them a commitment to support the work of this theme wherever possible within their classrooms.

5. He divided his class of thirty-one students into four heterogeneous groups, which formed the individual Learners' Circles. A timetable was posted to indicate when each Circle was to work in the library and when it was to meet with him.

6. He examined students' work portfolios to see what they knew and what they needed to review or learn. He decided they could all, with varying degrees of proficiency, re-tell and write from another point of view; however, from his notes on previous group and class discussions, he felt they needed additional

experience to understand more complex cause-and-effect relationships. He decided to use the discussions in the Learners' Circles to help the students identify moral dilemmas and issues present in most science-fiction work and relate them to their own lives. "We looked at universal truths in the light of current situations."

7. His planning now included the students. Together they brainstormed what they already knew about science fiction, recording their results on a chart. They devised an evaluation scheme where 25 percent of their mark would be based on the results of a written test and the remaining 75 percent on individual assignments and group presentations. The teacher, student and peers would be involved in the assessment procedure for this 75 per cent.

What is science fiction?

aliens
space travel
Star Trek , E.T.
futuristic - teaches you about future states
mutants
advanced technology
new places & beings, planets, life forms
fantasy, not real
discovery of the unknown
things that could happen but probably won't
Star Wars
robots in the future
computer technology
science - has some scientific truth
could teach a lesson - Don't play God
educational - teaches values

Immersion

This phase of the work took two weeks. Some activities were accomplished as a whole class, some in the Learners' Circles and some independently. Activities the teacher did with the class during the immersion phase of this theme are outlined here.

1. He opened with an overview of the history of science fiction, its main trends and styles of writing. He began with the work of Jules Verne and H.G. Wells and ended with Monica Hughes.

2. He showed *Forbidden Planet* to the class to whet their interest in the topic of science fiction. At the film's conclusion, students were required to work with a partner to record their thoughts and questions.

3. During the Learners' Circle the first week, students discussed these questions and thoughts. They also added information they had gleaned about science fiction to their initial brainstorming chart.

4. Each day he read to the students from a variety of resources, including the short story "A Wrinkle in Time" by Madeleine L'Engle, magazines, and comic strips in order to stimulate discussion about key elements of science-fiction work. Students added new information to their initial brainstorming chart. The teacher also used some of this time to identify and discuss moral issues.

5. The class attended a series of book talks at the library on available materials. Each student was required to select a book to read.

6. Time was given each day for the students to read their books. They logged their reading.

Reading Log			
Title of material read, viewed or heard	Date used	Circumstance of Use (alone, with peer(s) or teacher	Comment

The teacher took the opportunity during this first week to listen to the students read in order to ascertain that a suitable match had been made between the reader and the text. For those students who were using first-language materials, he enlisted the help of their Modern Language teachers.

7. In the second week, the students talked about key issues in their stories in the Learners' Circle. Any new information shared had to be substantiated with examples from the text, which were read aloud by the students. To facilitate this, the teacher gave each student a package of stick-on notes to mark the passage they intended to read and to jot down any thoughts or questions.

Response

This phase was scheduled to last three weeks. Each week, students had a list of activities to complete in any order they wished. It was their responsibility to complete all of the "musts" and at least one of the "choices" each week. The following chart helped many students organize their time and work.

Week One: Characters

Must	Choices (at least one)
meet once in the Learners' Circle	make a poster of the main character — use illustrations to indicate characteristics
work once in the library on the moral issue identified in your story and its implications for today or the immediate future	
	make a character profile
make one response journal entry in the voice of the protagonist	make a literary sociogram of the main characters
log daily reading	write an interview with one of the main characters

The students made their responses using their novels, materials shared in the large group or films they had viewed.

Week Two: Setting

Must	Choices (at least one)
meet once in the Learners' Circle	make a diorama/model of the setting
work once in the Library	make a poster of the setting
log daily reading	
make one response journal entry about the setting as it compares to present-day life	write a description of the setting
	tape a radio news report of earthlings arriving

Week Three: Conflict/Moral Issue

Must	Choices (at least one)
meet once in the Learners' Circle	make a bubble thinking chart of the two antagonists at a time of conflict
work once in the library	
log daily reading	offer a new ending that provides an alternative solution to the conflict; show pictorially one of the sources of conflict from your novel
write a new ending to one of the stories or films read to the class	

Included in the list of "musts" was a time each week when the students met with the teacher in the Learners' Circles. The focus of the discussions during these weeks is outlined here.

WEEK ONE

Students were asked in their individual groups to brainstorm on a chart:
• key characters a reader could expect to find in science-fiction material;
• generic characteristics of each character;
• ways that their actions influenced the drama.

Students were given the task of sketching a picture of a typical setting in a science-fiction novel. They labelled key elements.

WEEK THREE

Students were asked to list causes of conflict in their novels and their solutions. They explained, as a group, how these solutions could offer insights into resolutions of present-day problems.

The response phase of the theme, scheduled for three weeks, took five weeks to complete. Students were now ready to move on to the wrap-up phase.

Wrap-up

Activities in this phase are more intense and usually involve co-operative work. Together, students brainstormed ways in which they could show their understanding of the genre of science fiction. They decided they could:

- write a short science-fiction story;
- produce a science-fiction filmstrip;
- create a science-fiction comic strip;
- produce their own science-fiction video;
- role-play a moral issue and present a possible solution;
- build or draw a scene depicting a typical future setting — show how some present-day problems (e.g., crime, drugs, illness, pollution, extinction) were solved;
- research the work of a classic science-fiction author and compare it to the work of a more contemporary author.

Students selected partners with whom they wanted to work and decided on the wrap-up activity they wished to do. During the next two weeks, they worked hard on their responses. Time was spent in the Learners' Circles discussing how the work was going and practising their responses. At the end of this unit, students decided to share their work with their classmates and not with other groups in the school. They did agree, after much discussion, to put their finished products on display in the library for others to see.

The work was evaluated on three levels: self, group and teacher. Evaluation criteria for the first two types of evaluation were developed collaboratively with the students. For self-evaluation, students were asked to reflect on their learning and determine aspects that would benefit from change. The group evaluation had members of other Learners' Circles and the teacher use the form to evaluate the group's wrap-up presentation. On completion, consensus about final ratings was reached within the Learners' Circle and then with the teacher. Both evaluation forms are included on these pages.

Since many schools require teachers to give a formal written test or examination as part of the evaluation procedure, we have included our colleague's test, which is comprised of generic questions that relate to the broader learning outcomes of the thematic unit.

Self-Evaluation: Science Fiction

Name: _____ Class: _____ Date: _____

What do you know about science fiction now, compared with your previous understandings of this genre?

_____

_____

_____

What did you like about this unit of work? Why?

_____

_____

_____

What would you do differently next time? Why?

_____

_____

_____

Group-Product Evaluation: Science Fiction

Name: _____

Class: _____

Teacher: _____

Hours: _____ Date Started: _____ Date Completed: _____

Title or Description of Project: _____

Scale
1 = below average
2 = average
3 = above average
4 = outstanding

Product Evaluation

1. Originality and creativity of idea	1	2	3	4
2. Clarity and focus of presentation	1	2	3	4
3. Mastery of content	1	2	3	4
4. Level and sophistication of content	1	2	3	4
5. Care and attention to detail	1	2	3	4
6. Organization	1	2	3	4
7. Originality and variety of presentation	1	2	3	4
8. Value, interest, impact of the presentation on the audience	1	2	3	4

Adapted from *Independent Learning*, Ontario Secondary School Teachers' Federation, 1989.

Generic Questions for a Science-Fiction Test

Instructions

Select *one* of the following questions. Write a well-developed paragraph of 100-150 words consisting of a topic sentence that states the focus for your answer, a body in which you present *three* points to develop your viewpoint, along with references to the book, and finally, a concluding statement that summarizes the view expressed in the topic sentence.

1. Identify a central theme from a book you have read from the science-fiction theme. To what extent do you agree with the point of view expressed by the author? Make specific references to your text.

2. Define the specific problem or conflict identified in a book you have read from this theme. What were the causes of the problem? What were the effects produced by this problem? What was the solution offered by the author? Do you agree with the author's solution? Does it make sense? Why or why not?

or

Suggest possible solutions if the problem was not resolved in the novel.

3. How does the interplay between the human and alien characters in the story reflect multicultural issues in the world today?

Marking Scheme

10 — Content/ideas
 5 — Style (effective opening and concluding sentence; organization; sentence structure

Another Way to Begin — A Core-Study Unit on Ecology

A colleague who teaches science to grades seven and eight classes was frustrated by the use of the single resource that was provided. Many students were unable to understand the dense, content-laden science textbook and therefore were unable to participate successfully in classroom work. Instead of using the textbook, the teacher decided to use a thematic approach. "I noticed that the reading comprehension levels in my classroom varied greatly," she said. "Science textbooks that were appropriate to the topic were written in academic language that was unfamiliar to my students. I knew I needed to provide a range of resources if all students were to understand the work and be successful. I also knew, however, that there was a range of fiction materials, pamphlets, brochures and newspaper articles on the general topic of ecology that my students could read and understand. I decided that I would use these resources as a vehicle to assist my students to participate in this unit of study." She had several objectives as she planned this unit of work. She wanted:

- to provide all students with many opportunities to listen, speak, read, write, view and think about an issue that was relevant to them;
- to use this unit to teach students effective strategies to understand non-fiction materials;
- to help students develop feelings of concern and responsibility for the environment and to make them aware of the role they can play in protecting it.

She decided that a core-study format would best suit her objectives since she had only one month to explore the topic of ecology. She also knew from discussions with the teacher-librarian and the English teacher that the topic was still quite narrow; there were only a limited number of resources that were age-appropriate and offered varying readability levels. Like the focused-study format, the core-study format has four stages of development — planning, immersion, response and wrap-up.

Planning

During the planning phase of this theme, the teacher engaged in the following activities:

1. She arranged a meeting with the teacher-librarian to plan activities that would take place in the library. They agreed that during the immersion period, the teacher-librarian would give a book talk to introduce the students to available materials. The teacher-librarian also agreed to work with a different group of students each day during the wrap-up phase as they worked on group projects.
2. She held a meeting with the English teacher and the teacher-librarian to select appropriate resources. Together, they selected five short novels that were age-appropriate and offered a range of readability levels. The teacher arranged to borrow six copies of each of these short novels. They also selected a number of supplementary materials — picture books, magazines, pamphlets, newspapers, first-language materials and films.
3. With the teacher-librarian's help, she found a series of age-appropriate picture books to read to the class, as well as finding the film *The Man Who Planted Trees* for the class to view.
4. She examined the students' work portfolios and her records to determine the skills, knowledge and values they needed to review and learn. She decided that they had a lot of experience with notetaking and re-telling and could do these activities independently. As a group, however, they needed to develop and broaden their repertoire of strategies to understand non-fiction materials.
5. She now involved the students in the planning. Together they brainstormed what they knew about the topic of ecology and what questions they would like answered.
6. The students and teacher developed a collaborative evaluation scheme for this unit of work.

Immersion

The goal of this phase was to immerse the students in information about the topic. Scheduled to last for one six-day block of time with each period lasting 75 minutes, students took part in the following activities:

1. On the first day, the teacher read the picture book *The Man Who Planted Trees* by Jean Giono to the class to pique their interest in the topic. When she had finished, she divided the class into heterogeneous groups of four or five students. Students were asked to re-tell the story using the strategy described here. Students sat in a circle with one student designated to start the re-telling. After thirty seconds, the teacher clapped her hands and the student on the right picked up the story. This continued around the circle until the story was finished. During this time, the teacher moved around the room observing, listening and providing prompts where necessary. When they had finished, students were asked to write a group synopsis of the plot. A reporter from each group shared its version with the whole class. A class discussion of the reports followed, with each group given the opportunity to modify or add to their re-telling. The next day, students were asked to brainstorm in small groups and record the answers to the following questions:
   • Does this story have any relevance today? Why or why not?
   • What is one important idea the story made you think about?
     The groups then shared their responses and a combined chart was made. It was saved for future study.
2. The students visited the library to participate in a book talk given by the teacher-librarian on available materials. Four core novels were provided, as well as a range of magazines, pamphlets and newspapers. Each student was asked to select a novel or newspapers, magazines or pamphlets to use as an introduction to this unit of study. Those who selected the same novel formed a Learners' Circle that met once in a six-day cycle with the teacher. Students who selected newspapers, magazines or pamphlets formed another natural Learners' Circle. Over the course of the theme, students were required to be part of both a novel group and a newspaper, magazine or pamphlet group.
3. Students were given time each day to read their materials. They logged their reading and kept a record in their response journal of the main ecological issue, its causes and solutions. When they had finished reading one source, they selected another and continued reading, always looking for main issues.
4. The teacher, with the students, gathered materials for an attractive display that was placed in a corner of the classroom.

All supplementary books and magazines were housed there while a bulletin board was reserved for relevant articles.

5. The teacher showed the thirty-minute video, *The Man Who Planted Trees*. After viewing the video, students worked in groups to compare the video with the story.

Response

During this phase of the theme (10-12 75-minute periods), the teacher planned for whole-class, Learners' Circle and independent activities. In the whole-class time, she read from a variety of picture books and expository articles. The students and teacher developed a cumulative record of causes of ecological dangers and brainstormed possible preventive measures. She also used this time to teach the following strategy to help students use their prior knowledge to understand expository text.

An Expectation Guide

1. Have the group read the title of a short article found in a local newspaper.

2. Instruct the students to write, in point form, all information they already know about the topic.

3. Have the students develop two questions they hope the article will answer.

4. Assign students to cross-ability groups and have them read the article to determine if their information was accurate and their questions were answered. Record the information found in the form of answers to the questions that were raised prior to the reading.

5. Have the students share their work with the whole group.

The Rain forests last holdouts

- there arn't many rainforests left in the world
- the rainforests that are left are in remote areas with lots of disease, no technology.
- loggers cut down the trees and kill the forest
- miners mine for minerals and wreck the soil
- lots of people are fighting to make the rainforest into parks.
- some countries have laws to protect the forests
- when forests are destroyed people have to move and learn to live in cities.
- lots of people have been killed over the rainforest.

Two questions

1. Should the remaining rainforests be protected? Why? Why not?

2. Where are the remaining rainforests?

Group C – 9B

During the Learners' Circle time, the teacher took the opportunity to teach another strategy to help students understand expository information. She used a newspaper article to teach the students how to use an anticipation guide (see page 54 for steps to take).

Students were also required to work independently to complete the following activities:

1. They wrote two response journal entries based on their reading. For each entry, they identified main sources of conflict from their novel, presented opposing views and linked this conflict to one found in their community.
2. Students read every day and logged their reading.
3. Students met twice in the Learners' Circle.

In addition, they had to work with a partner to select and complete one of the following activities. Their choices were to:

- develop an anticipation guide for other students to use as they read an expository piece of text and to provide an answer sheet;
- make an expectation guide for one of the articles on the topic of ecology;
- design a poster that shows how an identified environmental danger can be averted;
- produce a crossword puzzle and an answer sheet using key words from the topic (crossword programs available for both the Macintosh and IBM computers).

Wrap-up

Students worked in small groups or with a partner to show their learning. From the following brainstormed possibilities, they selected an activity to demonstrate new understandings of the topic to their peers. Their choices were to:

- design a board game for younger children (see p. 55);
- create a diorama that shows a factual ecological disaster. Include cards to explain what was done to stop the disaster from spreading and an action plan to prevent such a disaster in the future;
- identify a danger to the environment. Design a commercial to help the public become aware of both the danger and steps that should be taken to avoid it;
- research a community ecological concern. Pose a question to be answered; for example, ''Should the government fund the

recycling of bottles and cans?" Take sides and prepare a debate to share with the class;

- brainstorm an environmental concern, for example, over-fishing, lumber stripping, water pollution, excessive garbage. Design a filmstrip that offers practical solutions to the problem.

Each day, the students worked in the library and the classroom preparing their responses. During this time, the teacher circulated throughout the room offering guidance, information, prompts, praise and encouragement. Time was spent in the Learners' Circle discussing how the work was progressing and practising sharing. At the end of this time, students organized a display of their work in the library. They invited other intermediate-level classes, their younger buddy readers and their parents to view the display. Groups stationed themselves at their display to explain their work. Students developed the following evaluation forms with their teacher to help them with their written work.

Self-Evaluation Strategies

Name: _____ Class: _____ Date: _____

1. Personal point of view
Underline the sentences that reflect your opinion.

2. Supporting arguments for this point of view
Underline two other sentences that support your point of view.

3. Other points of view
Underline other points of view you have presented and your response to these differing opinions.

4. Sequence and logic
Underline and number the sequence of ideas presented. Does this organization make sense?

5. Surface features
Are there errors in spelling, grammar and punctuation?

Peer-Evaluation Strategies

Name: _____ Class: _____ Date: _____
Evaluator: _____

1. The presenters clearly indicated their points of view.   1 2 3 4 5

2. The presenters offered other materials to support these viewpoints.   1 2 3 4 5

3. The presenters put forth more than one viewpoint and dealt effectively with these divergent viewpoints.   1 2 3 4 5

4. The project was organized in a clear and logical manner.   1 2 3 4 5

5. The presenters edited their work accurately.   1 2 3 4 5

Additional Strategies for Accessing Prior Knowledge and Making Predictions

Before introducing a language activity, students need opportunities to access prior knowledge and make predictions. This helps students focus their thinking and makes the activity more meaningful. The following strategies work effectively with language activities using expository text and are based on strategies developed by Dorsey Hammond.

STRATEGY ONE

This strategy works well when students have little or no prior knowledge about the topic.
a. Choose twelve to fifteen words or phrases from the text and arrange them randomly on paper.
b. Ask the students to work in small groups to organize the words into categories.
c. Have two groups of students compare their categories.
d. After comparing their findings, the groups can confirm or alter their categories.

Sort the following words into categories of your own choosing. Be prepared to defend your choices.

The Wild World In Danger

endanger	erode	wilderness	poachers
thriving	legislation	food	health remedies
species	illegal	legal	zoo
pets	jewellery	environmentalists	protect

The Poachers' categories

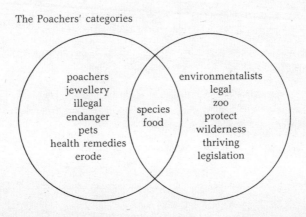

53

Our Response

people words	creature words	places words
• poachers	• pets	• wilderness
• environmentalists	• species	• zoo

things	doing words	gov't words
• jewellery	• endanger	• legal
• food	• erode	• illegal
	• protect	• legislation

STRATEGY TWO

This strategy works well with students who have some prior knowledge of the topic.

a. Prepare an anticipation guide that contains a number of statements on the topic. The statements may be true or false but they must be able to be verified by the text.

b. As a class, in small groups or individually ask students to indicate whether they agree or disagree with the statements on the anticipation guide.

c. After reading the material, have the students review the anticipation guide to determine which statements were true/false.

Sample Anticipation Guide

Based on the newspaper article "Scandal of Army Ivory Smugglers"

Despite a ban on the export of ivory and rhino horns, there is still a million pound 'ivory triangle' in southern Africa. **T F**

Units of the army are not involved in the smuggling of ivory and rhino horns across the Mozambique Border. **T F**

Elephants are only partially protected by the rules developed under the CTTES convention. **T F**

A report reveals only 55 elephants were killed by poachers in 1990, compared with 5,000 a year before the ban was introduced in 1989. **T F**

The elephant population in Kenya is slowly being rebuilt (20,000 in 1992). **T F**

Constructing Games

Games are a good way for students to show their understanding, as well as providing entertainment for both the creators and participators. These examples will provide your students with ideas for game design and perhaps launch them on a project involving the creation of new games for use in the classroom or in the home.

MEMORY GAMES

Readiness Steps
1. Have the students, in pairs or triads, brainstorm a series of questions and answers related to the theme.
2. Write questions on cards of the same color.
3. Write answers on cards of a different color.
4. Place all cards face down on the table.

To Play
1. Each player has an opportunity to turn over two cards. If the answer card answers the question card, the player may have another turn. If it does not, the cards must be put back in their exact place for the next player to test his or her memory and knowledge.
2. The player with the most pairs of cards at the end wins.

CO-OPERATIVE GAME

Readiness Steps
1. As a group, select a resource that involves conflict (e.g., environmental disaster, social problem).
2. Brainstorm ten or more obstacles to the solution of this conflict.
3. Brainstorm sixteen or more solutions for overcoming these obstacles.
4. Design a gameboard with fifty squares showing a path from start to finish.
5. Write obstacles on small cards and place them face-up on some of the squares.
6. Put the solutions to obstacles on cards.
7. Place the solution cards face down on the gameboard.
8. Construct a "rescuer" or a gamepiece that all players use.
9. Make dice.

To Play

1. The dealer passes solution cards to each player.
2. The first player rolls the dice and moves the rescuer the indicated number of spaces.
3. When an obstacle is reached, the player must put down a solution card. All players must agree with this solution.
4. If the player does not have a suitable card, another player can offer a solution. If no solution is found that is agreeable to all players, the game ends and the conflict is left unresolved.
5. If an agreeable solution is found, the next player rolls the dice. Play continues until the game is finished or the rescuer lands on a space containing a conflict that cannot be resolved.

CHAPTER SIX

Still Not Satisfied?

Our colleagues found, as have many other teachers, that thematic units of study within their subject discipline offer many advantages. They allow teachers to vary instruction, materials and student responses, embed mandated curriculum in a wider, more relevant context and offer students choice and responsibility for their learning, a condition identified by students and teachers alike as critical if true learning is to occur.

The more our colleagues used this framework of learning, however, the more frustrated they became by time constraints, overlapping but unco-ordinated curriculum themes and the realization that the work of one classroom was still not connected to the work of others. Learning continued to be isolated into small, segmented compartments.

Some schools have attempted to relieve the time frustration by moving to a semestered system or to a six-day cycle in which longer blocks of time are made available for individual subject learning. More time is provided for each subject discipline, but there is still no connection between learning in different subject areas. Learning continues to be divided into isolated compartments, often with duplication of skills. In addition, in some semestered systems there is a time gap between the offering of subjects. For example, history may be offered in the first semester of year one and the second semester of year two.

We suggest that a more effective way of alleviating time constraints and connecting the work of various disciplines is to seek out umbrella themes that fulfil mandated learning outcomes for each subject discipline. In this model, teachers work in collaboration and deliver the same broad theme in their classrooms.

Common Broad-Based Theme: Consecutive Delivery

To begin using a common theme, seek out colleagues who share a similar philosophy of teaching and learning, see a need for collaboration and change and understand and use a thematic framework in their subject areas. Negotiate a change in the timetable so the that the two subjects are timetabled back-to-back and are located in classrooms beside each other or in the same general location. Agree on a broad common theme that offers lots of student choice and fulfils prescribed learning outcomes of each subject discipline. Timetable common time for ongoing preparation, planning and evaluation.

One School's Story — A Core-Study Unit on Hazardous Wastes

Three teachers of grade nine history, science and English had introduced thematic units of work in their disciplines during the past year. They enjoyed the experience but were frustrated by the overlap and overload in curriculum delivery. They devised a pilot project in which they collaborated to provide a theme that would be of interest to students and allow them to fulfil mandated learning outcomes of each of their subject disciplines. They chose the topic of hazardous waste because it was current, provocative and covered required knowledge, skills and values. The teachers decided to plan jointly the unit of work but to work independently in their classrooms on this theme. They allotted six weeks for this project.

Planning

The three teachers decided on common experiences and activities they would offer the students in each class.
1. They agreed to provide experiences to help students:
   - understand the complexity of the issues involved;
   - appreciate other points of view;
   - identify bias in the media;
   - understand the function and structure of government regarding responsibilities, rights and policies;
   - design an environmentally friendly product.
2. They negotiated a timetable that allowed students to move through their classes in sequence and arranged a common

meeting time for ongoing discussions about the theme.

3. Each teacher collected a variety of resources, including relevant print and media material, articles, good literature of various genres, first-language books and current historical texts which present information from many viewpoints.
4. The teachers decided that during the wrap-up phase students would work in all three classes on one integrated project to demonstrate their learning about hazardous waste.
5. They divided their classes into varied ability groupings which were manageable for discussion. Each group would meet daily with the teacher in the Learners' Circle.
6. They rearranged the physical space of the classrooms to provide small-group workspaces and some storage space.

Immersion and Response

In this theme, teachers combined immersion and response stages to form one longer block of time. Whole-class, small-group and independent activities were planned.

In the English class, students were engaged in a variety of activities that were designed to heighten their interest in and deepen their understanding of the issues.

1. They brainstormed as a class what they thought the term "hazardous waste" meant and gave examples and causes.
2. The teacher read the picture book *The River Ran Wild* by Lynne Cherry to stimulate discussion.
3. Students listened to Pete Seeger's recording of "Sailin' Up, Sailin' Down," which celebrates the clean-up of the Hudson River.
4. Students selected a pamphlet or article on the topic from classroom or library resources, identified issues and wrote responses, which they shared in the Learners' Circle.
5. In the Learners' Circle, they identified common causes of hazardous waste from their articles. They began a cumulative chart.
6. They examined newspaper advertisements to identify strategies advertisers use to sell products.

In the history class, the teacher planned experiences that would complement those of the other subject disciplines.

1. She began with a short series of lectures on various levels of government, their responsibilities by law for the regulation of hazardous materials and the process used to pass a law.

2. She read the environmental story *The Kapok Tree* by Lynne Cherry to help set a context for students' understanding of issues. As well, she used this story to teach students how to write a letter that expresses a particular point of view. Together, the students brainstormed a list of information that such a letter should contain. She demonstrated the format of the letter using the information provided. Students were divided into groups of three and given the following task:
    • adopt the role of one of the characters in the story;
    • write a letter to the appropriate level of government expressing your point of view;
    • share this letter with the whole group for comments.
3. Each Learners' Circle was assigned the following research task:
    • identify an environmental concern;
    • use resources to provide a brief history of this concern;
    • identify issues and points of view held;
    • identify the level of government responsible for this concern. Research the identity and address of the politician responsible;
    • outline specific government responsibilities.

Students also worked at a variety of whole-group, small-group and independent activities in the science class.

1. Students brainstormed, as a whole group, characteristics of hazardous waste materials. Together, they read a pamphlet on hazardous waste before pairing up to compare their brainstormed ideas with information found in resource materials.
2. They learned how to design a survey. They examined several examples of surveys and in groups developed criteria for a good survey form.

Criteria for a Successful Survey

It must be easily understood.
It must give you the information you want.
It must be clearly designed so people will believe it is not hard to fill out.
It must be clear; the questions are easy to answer.
It must make allowances for people who can't read or write in English, French or any language (i.e., pictures or symbols that can be understood without the use of words).

---

3. Each Learning Circle was assigned this task. Using library, classroom and community resources, the group identified ten hazardous chemicals commonly found in the home. They designed a household survey and completed it in their homes. As a group, they made a common chart of the results.
4. In groups, students examined popular cleaning and personal hygiene materials. Using the information they had on hazardous materials, their task was to identify those products that contain potentially hazardous waste materials.
5. Each student was asked to identify a "home remedy" that was environmentally friendly and achieved the same results as hazardous materials (e.g., using baking soda to clean surfaces). Students were encouraged to share folk remedies from their, or their parents', country of origin.

Although the teachers had planned to spend only three weeks on these phases of the theme, the work took an additional two weeks because of students' intense involvement in learning. After this period, they were ready to move on to the final phase.

Wrap-up

The three teachers worked as a team in this phase. Students were given an opportunity to select one response that could be worked on in each of the three rooms. Together, the teachers and students agreed that the students would work individually, in pairs or in triads to design and construct or illustrate an environmentally friendly product. They could select one of the following options to market their product:
• design a bulletin board;
• prepare a display and oral presentation;
• develop and role-play a commercial;
• develop a video commercial;
• use the Hypercard program available on the Macintosh computer;
• write a letter to the appropriate level of government describing their product and offering reasons why it should be mandated by law as a substitute for a potentially hazardous one.

Bleach away is the way to go. No more messy spills . No more being afraid of smelling like a laundry room. Bleach Away is the first bleach that is environmentally friendly. It doesn't contain any harmful elements that normal bleaches contain. Bleach Away's only ingredient is Baking Soda. Natures natural cleaning product. Baking soda doesn't contain any harmful chemicals. The only ingredient baking soda contains is sodium bicarbanate. Sodium bicarbanate is a weak basic salt. And not only is the ingredients safe for the environment but, so is the packaging! Since Bleach Away is a powder, it doesn't need to be packaged in any form of plastic. Bleach Away's packaging is out of cardboard, which can be reycyled. If you care for your world, you will realize that Bleach Away is the only bleach that is environmentally safe!

Click for Picture of Product

BY SHABANA ISHMAIL 9D

Bleach Away | Card 2 of 2

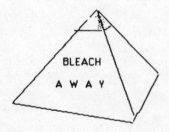

BLEACH AWAY
THE ONLY BLEACH
THAT IS ENVIRON-
MENTALLY SAFE.

Return to Description

62

At the end of this phase, students met as a group to share their products and evaluate their own and their peers' work. They displayed their work in the local library for the general public to examine. Teachers were enthusiastic about the quality of the work that their students displayed — ingenuity, creativity, logic and effective marketing strategies were in evidence. Time had been found in the crowded day and curriculum for the students to become immersed in a topic that was relevant to them and which connected work of one classroom to that of another. Academic learning held meaning for these students — they had opportunities to choose topics of interest and methods of demonstrating their thinking.

Attention: English and Science — A Focused-Study Unit on Survival

The following focused-study theme has been designed for use by English and science teachers.

Planning

As other theme outlines have shown, advance planning is essential to theme success. We have outlined suggested activities for this theme in order to help you establish clear expectations of learning outcomes and tasks to be explored.
1. Examine course guidelines of the two subjects to determine common and subject-specific learning outcomes.
2. Negotiate with the timetable committee for consecutive periods of study for the group of students participating in the theme. Also negotiate common preparation and evaluation times.
3. Arrange for rooms that are adjacent or close to each other.
4. Ask the teacher-librarian to locate a range of age-appropriate fiction and non-fiction materials that focus on the theme of survival — plant, animal and human. Include picture books, novels, pamphlets, magazines and newspapers (the last three are good sources of materials for students literate only in their first language).
5. Plan, with the teacher-librarian, activities that will take place in the library under his or her supervision.

6. Plan a series of activities for the immersion phase of this unit of work. Decide when and in which classroom they will take place.
7. Plan a series of choices for wrap-up activities that students can work on in the classroom and in the library.
8. Divide the class of thirty into five multi-ability groups. These groups will form the Learners' Circles. Plan to meet with one of these groups in each class every day. Devise a schedule and post it for easy reference.
9. Agree on the method and criteria for evaluation of this unit of work.

Immersion

This phase will likely take one to two weeks. Students have the opportunity to work in large and small groups, as well as working independently. Teachers can decide how to divide the activities for this phase.
1. Brainstorm with the students the meaning of the term "survival." Record students' ideas on a chart.
2. In groups, have students list factors that might influence the probability of survival. Share these brainstorming ideas and make one common chart. Post this chart in both rooms for future reference.
3. Select one of the following novels: *Marco* by Ann Turnbill, *Hatchet* by Gary Paulsen, *Slakes' Limbo* by Felice Holman, *The Girl with the White Flag* by Tomiko Higa or *My Name Is Not Angelica* by Scott O'Dell. Read this novel to the class every day.
4. Teach students how to use a dialectical notebook to help clarify their thinking about the text. These notebooks, documented in Ann E. Berthoff's *The Journal Book* (Boynton Cook/ Heinemann) are described on the next page.

Dialectical Notebooks

Provide each student with a notebook.

On the left-hand side of a spread, students make observations and sketches, note impressions and questions they have and copy passages or other responses as they read, listen or view.

On the right-hand side of a spread, students make notes based on their first set of notes and respond to the impressions, passages and other responses they made previously.

Survival In the Jungle - Susan Landman
Chapter three

ecosystem?	dictionary → "complex of a community and its environment functioning as a unit."
emergent level trees of 250 ft - what bend, how old?	· 25,000 different types - most have smooth light coloured bark.
canopy → reminds me of?	theater, our house at the back.
fungi? like ours?	- no - feeds trees, provides food.
how do people live? where?	N. Guinea tree people live in the tops of trees - other tribes live in remote villages, small groupings.
pygmies? - live in rainforest or die why?	sunlight makes them sick - like albinos?

5. Show one of the classic survival videos, for example, *Swiss Family Robinson* or *Robinson Crusoe*. Have the students use their dialectical notebooks to record their responses.
6. Visit the library for a book talk by the teacher-librarian on available materials. Have each student select something to read.
7. Schedule time each day for the students to read from the materials provided.
8. In both classes, meet daily with a different Learners' Circle to discuss the students' readings and entries in their dialectical notebooks.

Response

Allow two to three weeks for this phase. Activities have been identified for each classroom.

ENGLISH CLASS

Each day the teacher might:
- read to the class or view a film;
- schedule time for students to read from materials they have selected. Remind them to record their reading;
- meet with one of the Learners' Circles. At this time, have each student offer a short synopsis of the story with particular reference to factors that hindered or helped survival.

Each week students must make one entry in their dialectical notebook about their reading or viewing and complete one of the following response activities on the materials they have been reading.
1. Develop a literary sociogram that illustrates relationships between main characters.
2. Create a profile of the main character, showing characteristics that allowed this person to survive.
3. Design an advertisement to sell the book.
4. Retell main events of the story in comic-book form.
5. Select two books; compare and contrast reasons for characters' survival.
6. Construct a game that shows the main character's journey and the obstacles she or he had to overcome to survive.

1. Using the chart developed in the immersion phase of this unit of work, students identify factors that affect survival of plants (temperature, light, soil, water).
2. Give each Learners' Circle several packages of mung beans. Assign each group a task from the following list and make up a condition for their work:
   - using the condition assigned, develop a hypothesis about the most favorable environment for the beans' survival;
   - design a series of experiments that will prove the hypothesis. Keep conditions constant;
   - record conditions for each experiment;
   - record any changes each day;
   - at the end of two weeks, compare results.

   Each group shares results of the experiments with the class. Students, using this information, make a prediction about the most favorable conditions for the survival of mung beans. In each Learners' Circle, they test this hypothesis.
3. Provide each Learners' Circle with an article or pamphlet on an extinct species (e.g., dinosaurs, woolly mammoth). Using this information, students develop a chart that offers reasons why this species didn't survive.

Wrap-up

This phase will last for two to three weeks. Have students brainstorm areas of interest they would like to pursue. Ask them to work in pairs or triads. Schedule time in both classes for students to work on their responses. Teachers' roles during this phase are critical — they are needed to provide further instruction, to extend learning, to ask probing questions and to help students present their learning in as clear and interesting a manner as possible.

Here are some sample wrap-up activities.

1. Identify a race of people or a breed of mammals, insects, water creatures, birds or plants that is now extinct. Research causes for this extinction. Present findings to the class using a display, filmstrip, model, video, and so on. Offer an opinion as to how this extinction could have been prevented. Are there instances when certain species must be controlled or eliminated? Why or why not?

2. Identify a race of people or a breed of animals, mammals, insects, birds, water creatures or plants that was on the verge of extinction but has survived. Research the causes of this survival. Present findings to the class using a display, filmstrip, book, oral presentation, and so on.
3. Identify a plant species or breed of wildlife that needs to be controlled. Present arguments about why this control is necessary. Research methods of control and comment on their merits. Present findings to the class using a display, filmstrip, model, video, and so on.
4. Collect a number of picture books that deal with the extinction of a breed of animals, wildlife or people. Examine these materials to determine strategies that authors and illustrators use to convey their ideas to younger students. Write and illustrate a book on some aspect of survival or extinction. Read the book to younger children to gauge their reaction before publishing the book in its final form. Present the book and the reaction it received from younger children to the class.

The following evaluation form helps students to evaluate the performance of their group as well as their performance within the group.

Group and Self-Evaluation

Names: _____

Evaluator: _____ Date: _____ Class: _____

	Low	Moderate	High

How satisfied do you feel about the
group at this moment?   1 2   3   4   5

How satisfied are you with the amount
and quality of your participation in the
group?   1 2   3   4   5

To what extent were your opinions and
thoughts asked for and valued in the
group?   1 2   3   4   5

How open and free were you to express
your thoughts?   1 2   3   4   5

How clear were your group's goals?   1 2   3   4   5

How effective were you in helping your
group to reach its goals?   1 2   3   4   5

How committed was the group to facing
its problems?   1 2   3   4   5

From *Linking Evaluation with Learning in Science*, The
Metropolitan Toronto School Board, 1989.

CHAPTER SEVEN
Almost There!

Despite enthusiasm about the benefits of working with colleagues, continuity of programming from one classroom to the next and relevancy of the work for students, teachers found the consecutive model of delivery was not without problems. Frustrated by structural constraints, many were unable to negotiate exclusive use of a suitable room. Lack of a constant space made it difficult for students to work over time on a variety of responses and to carry on with one project in all three classes. Some teachers also had difficulty restructuring the timetable so that classes could take place in sequence and sufficient time be allowed for ongoing preparation and evaluation. For those teachers who negotiated the exclusive use of a suitable room, necessary resources were often housed in subject discipline classrooms or workrooms, located far from the work of the shared classroom.

Teachers with experience in planning common themes recommend that two teachers are a realistic number to plan, implement and evaluate successfully. Three or four teachers are too wieldy a team, making it difficult to timetable and plan common ongoing preparation and evaluation times. Teachers have also learned that not all subjects can be integrated for all themes. Language learning, for the most part, is the easiest to integrate, as it is a vehicle for all content learning.

In all instances, students moved from one teacher to another, making it difficult to establish the all-important learner-teacher bond of trust. In response to this need, some schools have established an advisor-advisee program in which time is set aside each day for a teacher to meet with a constant group of students. While this move is well-intentioned, it has several drawbacks: it's often artificial; it's not connected to other learning; students may form a bond with a teacher who is not offering them instruction; and time is limited for delving into topics of substance.

We suggest, then, that the creation of broad integrated thematic units of work, delivered by one or two teachers offers students the best opportunity to become truly engaged learners. There are several reasons for this: they allow learners the necessary time to become immersed in the learning; they connect the work of one classroom to another; and they allow students the chance to form a bond with one teacher who is involved in their learning. In this model, one or two teachers would deliver an integrated curriculum to a constant group of students. This curriculum would encompass the work of individual subject disciplines.

An Integrated History and English Theme — A Focused-Study Unit on Immigration

Two teachers in a destreamed intermediate setting decided that they were going to work together to deliver a common integrated history and English unit of work. Over the past year, they had worked successfully on a number of joint themes but were frustrated by the revolving groups of students that went through their classrooms. In order to cut down on the number of students they saw each day, they decided to pilot an integrated theme. During this period of time, each would teach one group of students a unit of work that would encompass learning outcomes of both history and English curricula. For the remainder of the day, they taught their subject disciplines to changing groups of students.

Together, they decided that they could develop a thematic unit of work on immigration that would meet objectives of both subject disciplines. They knew that the theme would be of interest and relevance to students as many were recent immigrants — their experiences would form the basis for understanding more abstract concepts of the topic. By using a thematic structure, teachers provided students with opportunities to see connections between their experiences and classroom work.

Planning

The teachers developed a co-operative plan where each had equal opportunity to shape the theme's development. Both teachers were aware of the need to cover the required curriculum for their course.

1. The history teacher examined the learning outcomes of her grade nine course of study. Students were expected to have an understanding of the following topics: government, democracy, citizenship and basic conflicts and problems facing the country from the 1900s to today.
2. The English teacher determined that students were expected to be able to generate and rank questions, find sources of information, discuss reliability and meaning, record, summarize and synthesize information, and assess and apply information. Students were also required to display an understanding of various genres through the study of character, plot and setting.
3. Together, the teachers decided that through theme work they could achieve the following common learning outcomes. They shared these learning outcomes with the students at the beginning of the theme, posting them in the classrooms for easy reference.

Learning Outcomes for Immigration Themes

(a) The students are involved in the topic; they take part in the discussions and assigned activities.
(b) The students are able to connect the new learnings to previous experiences and understandings.
(c) The students are able to use language to communicate their thinking effectively.
(d) The students demonstrate a value system and can respond in a positive way to other value systems.

The teachers also decided on the criteria that they would be using to evaluate individual student performances. Like the learning outcomes, these criteria were posted for reference.

Evaluation Criteria for Immigration Theme

(a) The student contributes readily during discusssions.
(b) The student generates questions and researches answers independently.
(c) The student locates, selects and uses information purposefully.
(d) The student makes notes that summarize, organize and record important information.

(e) When answering questions, the student links information to other areas of the curriculum and demonstrates an awareness of patterns, and offers interpretations that go beyond the text.

(f) The student can argue persuasively and reflect a personal viewpoint which is supported with detail.

(g) The student displays an understanding of various points of view.

(h) The student responds to the learning in a variety of ways, for example, through art, music, drama, construction, writing and speaking.

(i) The student demonstrates an understanding of the conventions of language, that is, grammar, spelling, punctuation and form.

4. They examined students' portfolios and their records to assess knowledge, skills and values that needed to be taught or reviewed.

5. They met with the teacher-librarian who helped them locate relevant print and media materials, articles, good literature of various genres, first-language books and current historical texts that present information from many viewpoints.

6. They searched out and contacted community members, authors and experts who could speak to their group. (A local senior citizens' complex proved to be an excellent resource.)

7. They negotiated with the school's timetable committee for:
   • ongoing shared planning and evaluation meeting times;
   • concurrent double-period class teaching times;
   • two rooms for their exclusive use.

8. They rearranged the room to include space for large-group activities, small-group work areas and storage space.

9. They divided each class into heterogeneous ability groups that were of a manageable size for discussion.

Immersion

The teachers allotted two weeks for immersion activities. The following overview provides a comprehensive listing of their work during this period.

1. They brainstormed with the students in each class what they thought the term "immigration" meant. They compared this brainstorming as a combined group.

2. Each day both teachers selected a story from the anthology,

The Story of Canada by Janet Lunn and Christopher Moore, and read it to the class. Each class made a cumulative chart of the people who came to Canada and some of their reasons for emigrating.

3. The students visited the library for a book talk by the teacher-librarian about the available materials. Each student was asked to select a novel to read.
4. Time was scheduled each day for the students to read their novels. Students logged their reading and made one reading response journal entry each week.
5. Teachers taught the class as a whole how to devise a questionnaire. In groups, the students decided what information about immigration should be included. Each group devised specific questions they would use with their families or friends, for example, "Why did you or your ancestors emigrate?" "What made life easier on arrival?" "What difficulties were encountered?"
6. They invited members of the community to the classrooms to share their stories. For some sessions, the two classes met together.

Response

For each of the four weeks of this phase, students were required to schedule time for daily reading and to meet once with the teacher in the Learners' Circle. Over this time, they were also required to choose and complete one general activity and one activity based on their novel.

GENERAL ACTIVITIES

1. Using the questionnaire developed in class, interview family members about their journey to Canada. Share this information with other members of your small group and make a common chart of the responses.
2. Design a poster to encourage new immigrants to come to one area of the country — the west coast, the east coast, the north, and so on.
3. Make a diorama of what life was like on arrival for yourself or your ancestors.

NOVEL ACTIVITIES

1. Make a timeline of the main character's journey.

2. Adopt the role of one of the main characters. Write a letter to a friend telling about your voyage and your feelings as you arrived at your new home or write a letter to a friend telling how you felt when the new immigrants arrived.
3. Assume the role of one of the main characters. Retell significant events of the story in the form of diary entries.
4. Take on the role of a newspaper reporter and develop five questions to ask the new arrivals. Select your best question and answer it.
5. Draw the scene that the main character sees as she or he leaves his or her home or as she or he arrives in the new land.
6. Select a scene in which the main character either leaves his or her old home or arrives at his or her destination. Illustrate this scene. Use speech bubbles for the dialogue and thought bubbles for thoughts. Compare the spoken words with the thoughts.
7. Select a place, practice or person about which you want to know more. Use classroom and library resources for your research. Present findings to your small group.
8. Create a literary sociogram of the characters.

LEARNERS' CIRCLE ACTIVITIES

1. Have students identify the main characters from their novel, the reasons they left their homes, the places they went to, and the events that happened when they arrived. Ask them to look for commonalities.
2. Ask the students to use a literary sociogram to explore relationships between characters. Use a picture book such as *Angel Child, Dragon Child*.
3. Ask the students how to make a bubble thinking response.

The response phase of this unit took four weeks to complete as some students became very involved in their responses. During this time, the two classes worked independently for the most part, coming together when viewing films or sharing stories. The classes were now ready to move on to the final phase of this theme.

Wrap-up

The teachers allocated two weeks of intense study for this phase of the work. Students had the option to work in pairs, in triads or in small groups and could do their research and response in the library or one of the two classrooms. The two teachers and the teacher-librarian acted as resources during these sessions, moving among groups of students offering advice, prompts, encouragement and clarification. Students were given the option of completing one of the following activities or designing an area of independent study.

1. Use your own or your ancestors' experiences as an immigrant or a Native person as the foundation for research on the history of your ethnic group in this country. Present your information in one of the following ways:
   • a filmstrip;
   • a display and oral presentation;
   • a booklet;
   • a slide and tape.
2. Research services available to assist new immigrants. Design a pamphlet or a short video in first language that informs new arrivals of these services.
3. Discuss the immigration history of the members of your group. Use this information to begin to develop a timeline for this country's immigration. Start no later than the early 1800s.
4. Decide on any decade of this country's history. Research life in your area during that decade — who lived here, who held power, why people came, what life was like. Present your research in one of the following ways:
   • a filmstrip;
   • a model and oral presentation;
   • a mural and written explanation;
   • a slide and tape show.
5. Research the form that successful picture books take. Using this information, create a picture book for young children that deals with the difficulties and uncertainties of leaving homelands.

When the students had completed their areas of study, they met to share their work with the whole group. The teacher, with the students, reviewed the evaluation criteria they had discussed during the planning stage of the theme and critiqued their work. They also displayed their work in the library for parents and other classes to view. Each group of students was responsible for staffing the display and answering questions.

This was a very successful unit of work and was, as José said, "All about me! I had something to offer. I've been there!"

Social and Racial Justice: Ideas for Another Core-Study Unit

Like other themes outlined in this book, the theme of social and racial justice is an interesting one for many students, and provides plenty of avenues for pursuing areas of special interest. The outline of this theme study deviates from others given in this book — instead of providing a step-by-step outline of each of the four phases, we have provided large- and small-group, pair and independent activity suggestions for immersion, response and wrap-up work.

Immersion Activities

1. Brainstorm with the students the term "justice." Develop a cumulative chart of their responses.
2. During whole-class time, view a segment of the video *Many Voices* or *Cindy*. After viewing, have the students write their reactions, questions and feelings in their response journals.
3. During whole-class time, also read excerpts from resources, including historical texts, magazines, newspapers and novels that feature instances of injustice. Look for possible causes of injustice or unfairness and record them on charts.
4. One way we identify others is to label them. Brainstorm examples of various labels (e.g., soup label, aspirin label, chocolate bar label). Discuss why labels on products are useful. Ask students to determine why labels are less useful in describing people (e.g., less flexibility, describe only one dimension). Have students brainstorm labels they have heard applied to people. Discuss the fairness and logic of this practice.
5. For homework, have students watch television for one hour and log who they have seen and under what circumstances. Discuss the patterns they observed.
6. Divide the class into groups of five to six members. Provide each group with a collection of magazines and newspapers. Ask each group to select one section of the newspaper and create a collage using the illustrations, photos, headlines and words to represent the images found in that section. Students

share these collages and discuss patterns. Pose the question, "Is this justice? Why or why not?"

7. Have each student select from available materials a novel, magazine or pamphlet to read. Schedule time each day for the students to read and maintain their logs.

8. Meet each day with a different Learners' Circle group to discuss readings and teach students strategies for skimming non-fiction materials. Use an overhead and current newspaper articles for this demonstration.

Response Activities: Learners' Circles

1. Provide groups with a variety of pictures that show people in conflict. Have them examine the pictures and describe what is happening in each picture. Discuss underlying causes of conflict in terms of social and racial inequality.

2. Have students discuss stories they are reading. As they read, provide stick-on notes for them to jot down points they wish to make to the group. Open the discussion with the invitation, "Tell us about your book."

3. Have students bring books they are reading and place them on the table. From this collection, each student selects a book they have not read. From an examination of the front and back covers, they list all the possible social issues that might be addressed in the book. They test these predictions for accuracy with the student who brought the book to the Learners' Circle.

4. Have students keep an ongoing list in their response journal of instances of injustice or unfairness and the causes of these injustices. Ask them to compare these sources of inequality and create broad categories of the sources.

5. Ask each Learners' Circle member to share ways in which inequality in their reading was handled. The group compiles a list of actions that can be taken by students to change situations of inequality to situations of equality.

Response Activities: Independent and Pair Situations

Using the materials the students have read as a resource, ask them to select one of the following activities to complete.

1. Create a character profile. Share this work with your Learners' Circle.

2. Make two opposing silhouettes, one for reality and one for assumptions made about the character as the story unfolds.

Add appropriate words to the inside of the character to show differences between assumptions held and reality. Share this work with other members of your Learners' Circle.

3. Make a bubble-thinking response. Share this work with other members of your Learners' Circle.

4. Create a literary sociogram. Share this literary sociogram with other members of your Learners' Circle.

5. Design a thought journal bookmark. Outline one of the characters on a piece of stiff cardboard. As a friend reads, ask him or her to write on the book mark their thoughts and feelings about one of the main or subordinate characters. Ask him or her to describe what happened in the story that has led him or her to feel as she or he does.

6. Write frequently in your response journal. Select issues to respond to or use one of the following thought-starters.

I hope_____

I know _____

I think one of the problems is _____

I think a solution would be _____

I wonder _____

Using the resources you have selected, choose one of the following activities to complete.

1. Sketch a map that includes the major towns, cities, places, borders and rivers mentioned in your materials. Show a footstep progression naming the places the main character or characters visited in the correct order. Include a legend. Share this work with your Learners' Circle.

2. Illustrate each episode or chapter of the story you are reading or has been read to you. Write a synopsis or caption for each episode or chapter. Share this work with your Learners' Circle.

3. Select a place, person or time from your reading to research. Use library resources to present a mini-project on this topic.

Wrap-up Activities

For this period of time, students work in pairs, triads or small groups. Ask them to select one or more of the following activities.

1. Locate and clip words from the newspaper to form a headline that tells something about an injustice about which you have read, viewed or heard. Write a brief news story telling the facts of this story. Your editor has limited you to 50 words.

Remember to include who, what, where, when, why, how and a picture.

2. Design a conflict game with a partner or a small group. Begin by brainstorming a series of situations from your own lives that cause conflict. Put these problems on file cards. To play the game, place all the cards in a pile face down in the middle of the table. The first player picks up a card, reads it to the group and offers a solution to the problem. The rest of the group votes on the solution when the player says, ''Ready, set, vote.'' To vote ''yes,'' make a thumbs-up sign; to vote ''no,'' make a thumbs-down sign. ''No'' votes are subtracted from ''Yes'' votes to get each individual's points. The player with the most points wins.

3. Using newspapers and magazines, create a scrapbook about teenagers as depicted by the media. Prepare a short talk on this coverage — its content, accuracy, fairness and possible rationale. Present your views in letter form to the appropriate newspaper editor or columnist.

4. Write and perform a poem or rap complete with appropriate props that comments on some aspect of social or racial injustice.

5. Select a current source of controversy and prepare arguments for both sides of the question. Present a mock trial, complete with judge, attorneys and jury.

Each time teachers select this theme, they are amazed at the wealth of information, opinions and involvement demonstrated by their students. They have much to contribute as issues of fairness are paramount to their lives. This theme offers students opportunities to make connections to their own lives, to their learning in school and to the broader global society.

Conclusion

We have provided our plan for the integration of curriculum for young adolescents. A holistic curriculum enables students to make sense of their world. Broad-based thematic units that are global and socially relevant cross and connect subject disciplines and allow students to create meaning from learning, as well as enabling them to see patterns and connections in whole systems. In this way, students can better understand today's world and that of the future.

We believe teachers can and do make the difference. It is our opinion that all teachers and students want maximum opportunities for success in schools. Often, however, the structures in which we find ourselves become barriers to that success. By recognizing and collectively working to remove these disabling barriers, and by sharing quality interactions and curricula with students, teachers can truly create conditions for success. Enjoy.

Professional Resources

Cambourne, B. (1988). *The Whole Story*. Auckland, NZ: Ashton-Scholastic.

Chambers, A. (1991). *The Reading Environment*. Stroud, UK: Thimble Press.

Cummins, J. (1989). *Empowering Minority Students*. Sacramento: California Association for Bilingual Education.

Graham, N., & George, J. (1992). *Marking Success*. Markham, ON: Pembroke.

Harste, J., & Short, K. (1988). *Creating Classrooms for Authors*. Portsmouth, NH: Heinemann.

Hart-Hewins, L., & Wells, J. (1992). *Read It in the Classroom! Organizing an Interactive Language Arts Program, Grades 4-9*. Markham, ON: Pembroke/Portsmouth, NH: Heinemann.

Jobe, R., & Hart, P. (1991). *Canadian Connections. Experiencing Literature with Children*. Markham, ON: Pembroke.

Johnson, T., & Louis, D. (1989). *Literacy through Literature*. Portsmouth, NH: Heinemann/Richmond Hill, ON: Scholastic.

Parkin, F., & Sidnell, F. (1992). *ESL Is Everybody's Business*. Markham, ON: Pembroke.

Bibliography: Science Fiction

Asimov, I. (1969). *Foundation*. New York, NY: Bantam Books.

Asimov, I. (1971). *David Starr, Space Ranger*. Toronto: New American Library of Canada.

Bradbury, R. (1966). *S Is for Space*. New York: Doubleday.

Bradbury, R. (1969). *R Is for Rocket*. New York, NY: Bantam.

Bradbury, R. (1983). *The Illustrated Man*. New York, NY: Bantam.

Bradbury, R. (1984). *The Martian Chronicles*. New York, NY: Bantam.

Christopher, J. (1967). *The White Mountains*. New York, NY: Macmillan.

Clarke, A. (1963). *Childhood's End*. Orlando, FL: Harcourt Brace Jovanovich.

Clarke, A. (1968). *2001: A Space Odyssey*. New York, NY: New American Library/Dutton.

Clarke, A. (1990). *Rendezvous with Rama*. New York, NY: Bantam.

Crichton, M. (1991). *Jurassic Park*. New York, NY: Ballantine.

Danzinger, P. (1987). *This Place Has No Atmosphere*. New York, NY: Dell.

De Weese, G. (1985). *Black Suits from Outer Space*. New York, NY: Putnam.

De Weese, G. (1989). *The Calvin Nullifier*. New York, NY: Dell.

De Weese, G. (1989). *The Dandelion Caper*. New York, NY: Dell.

Duane, D. (1989). *My Enemy, My Ally*. New York, NY: Pocket Books.

Duane, D. (1991). *The Wounded Sky*. New York, NY: Pocket Books.

Godfrey, M. (1984). *Alien Wargames*. Richmond Hill, ON: Scholastic.

Heinlein, R. (1985). *Have Space Suit, Will Travel*. New York, NY: Ballantine.

Hoover, H.M. (1986). *The Lost Star*. New York, NY: Puffin.

Hughes, M. (1981). *The Guardian of Isis*. Markham, ON: Butterworths.

Hughes, M. (1982). *Ring-Rise, Ring-Set*. Markham, ON: Butterworths.

Hughes, M. (1982). *The Tomorrow City*. Scarborough, ON: Nelson.

Hughes, M. (1989). *The Isis Pedlar*. Markham, ON: Butterworths.

Hughes, M. (1989). *The Promise*. Don Mills, ON: Stoddart.

Hughes, M. (1990). *Invitation to the Game*. Toronto, ON: Harper Collins.

Hughes, M. (1991). *The Keeper of the Isis Light*. Markham, ON: Butterworths.

Hughes, M. (1992). *Sandwriter*. Don Mills, ON: General

Mackay, C. (1984). *The Minerva Program*. Toronto, ON: Lorimer.

Martel, S. (1982). *The City Underground*. Toronto, ON: Groundwood.

O'Brien, R. (1987). *Z for Zachariah*. New York, NY: Macmillan.

Pinkwater, D. (1980). *Fat Men from Space*. New York, NY: Dell.

Pinkwater, D. (1983). *The Snarkout Boys and the Avocado of Death*. New York, NY: New American Library/Dutton.

Pinkwater, D. (1985). *The Snarkout Boys and the Baconburg Horror*. New York, NY: New American Library/Dutton.

Pinkwater, D. (1987). *The Muffin Fiend*. New York, NY: Bantam.

Pinkwater, D. (1988). *Lizard Music*. New York, NY: Bantam.

Bibliography: Ecology

Core Novels

Craighead George, J. (1991). *Who Really Killed Cock Robin? An Ecological Mystery*. New York, NY: Harper Trophy.

Oppel, K. (1992). *Dead Water Zone*. Toronto, ON: Kids Can Press.

Paulsen, G. (1987). *Tracker*. New York, NY: Macmillan.

Smucker, B. (1987). *Jacob's Little Giant*. Toronto, ON: Penguin.

Supplementary Books

Allen, J. (1989). *Awaiting Developments*. London, UK: Walker.

Anderson, C. (1988). *Serpent's Tooth*. New York, NY: St. Martin's Press.

Baily, D. (1991). *What Can We Do About Wasting Water*. New York, NY: Franklin Watts.

Baines, J. (1992). *Oceans: Our Green World*. Hove, UK: Wayland.

Baines, J., & James, B. (1991). *This Fragile Earth*. New York, NY: Simon & Schuster.

Bellamy, D. (1988). *Our Changing World Series*. New York, NY: Simon & Schuster.

Blashfield, J.F., & Black, W.B. (1991). *Global Warming*. Chicago, IL: Children's Press.

Blashfield, J.F., & Black, W.B. (1991). *Recycling*. Chicago, IL: Children's Press.

Challand, H.J. (1991). *Vanishing Forests*. Chicago, IL: Children's Press.

Challand, H.J. (1992). *Disappearing Wetlands: Saving Planet Earth*. Chicago, IL: Children's Press.

Cherry, L. (1990). *The Great Kapok Tree: A Tale of the Amazon Rain Forest*. Orlando, FL: Harcourt Brace Jovanovich.

Cherry, L. (1992). *A River Ran Wild*. Orlando, FL: Harcourt Brace Jovanovich.

Cochrane, J. (1987). *Land Ecology*. Hove, UK: Wayland.

Farley, W. (1991). *The Black Stallion Series*. New York, NY: Knopf.

Gates, R. (1982). *Conservation*. Chicago, IL: Children's Press.

Giono, Jean. (1989). The Man Who Planted Trees. Toronto, ON: CBC Enterprises.

Godkin, C. (1989). *Wolf Island*. Markham, ON: Fitzhenry & Whiteside.

Hare, T. (1991). *Habitat Destruction*. New York, NY: Franklin Watts.

James, B. (1990). *Conserving Our World Series: Waste and Recycling*. Madison, NJ: Raintree/Steck-Vaughn.

Suzuki, D., & Hehner, B. (1989). *Looking at the Environment*. Don Mills, ON: Stoddart.

Smucker, B. (1992). *White Mist*. Toronto, ON: Penguin.

Van Allsberg, C. (1990). *Just a Dream*. Boston, MA: Houghton Mifflin.

Bibliography: Hazardous Waste

Cherry, L. (1992). *A River Ran Wild*. Orlando, FL: Harcourt Brace Jovanovich.

Gano, L. (1991). *Our Endangered Planet Series: Hazardous Waste*. San Diego, CA: Lucent Books.

Goldberg, J. (1993). *Economics and the Environment*. New York, NY: Franklin Watts.

Hare, T. (1991). *Save Our World Series: Toxic Waste*. New York, NY: Franklin Watts.

Hawkes, N. (1991). *Toxic Waste and Recycling*. New York, NY: Gloucester Press.

Jenkins, G.H. (1991). *Toxic Waste Troubled Society*. Vero Beach, FL: Rouke Corp. Inc.

Lucas, E. (1991). *Acid Rain*. Chicago, IL: Children's Press.

Schwartz, M. (1993). *The Environment and the Law: Earth at Risk*. New York, NY: Chelsea House.

Kits

Hazardous Waste Educational Resource Kit
Available from:
Federation of Ontario Naturalists
355 Lesmill Road
Don Mills ON M3B 2W8
(416) 444-8419

Hazardous Waste and You: A Teacher's Guide
Available from:

Ontario Waste Management Corporation
2 Bloor Street West, 11th Floor
Toronto, ON M4W 3E2
(416) 923-2918

* Contact your local environmental department for additional information.

Bibliography: Survival

Anderson, C. (1988). *Serpent's Tooth*. New York, NY: St. Martin's Press.

Anonymous. (1976). *A Real Diary: Go Ask Alice*. New York, NY: Avon.

Avi. (1991). *Windcatcher*. New York, NY: Macmillan

Bell, W. (1989). *Crabbe*. Don Mills, ON: General.

Cleary, B. (1984). *Dear Mr. Henshaw*. New York, NY: Dell.

Craighead George, J. (1974). *Julie of the Wolves*. New York, NY: Harper Trophy.

Fox, P. (1993). *Monkey Island*. New York, NY: Dell.

Gardiner, J.R. (1980). *Stone Fox*. New York, NY: HarperCollins.

Gutman, C. (1991). *The Empty House*. Woodchester, UK: Turton & Chambers.

Hest, A. (1993). *Love You Soldier*. New York: NY: Macmillan.

Heuck, S. (1988). *The Hideout*. New York, NY: Dutton.

Higa, T. (1992). *The Girl with the White Flag*. New York, NY: Dell.

Hill, K. (1990). *Toughboy and Sister*. New York, NY: Macmillan.

Holman, F. (1986). *Slake's Limbo*. New York, NY: Alladin.

Hughes, M. (1984). *Hunter in the Dark*. New York, NY: Avon.

Lingard, J. (1990). *Tug of War*. New York, NY: Dutton.

Lingman, M. (1991). *Sammy's Residential School*. Waterloo, ON: Penumbra.

Major, K. (1991). *Far from the Shore*. Don Mills, ON: Stoddart.

Martel, S. (1982). *The City Underground*. Toronto, ON: Groundwood.

Mazer, H. (1991). *Someone's Mother Is Missing*. New York, NY: Dell.

O'Brien, R. (1987). *Z for Zachariah*. New York, NY: Macmillan.

O'Dell, S. (1990). *My Name Is Not Angelica*. New York, NY: Dell.

Paulsen, G. (1987). *Dogsong*. New York, NY: Puffin.

Paulsen, G. (1988). *Hatchet*. New York, NY: Puffin.

Paulsen G. (1990). *The Island*. New York, NY: Dell.

Pinkwater, D. (1992). *Wingman*. New York, NY: Bantam.

Rostkowski, M.I. (1988). *After the Dancing Days*. New York, NY: HarperCollins.

Taylor, M.D. (1984). *Roll of Thunder, Hear My Cry*. New York, NY: Bantam.

Turnbill, A. (1990). *Maroo of the Winter Caves*. Boston, MA: Clarion.

Uchida, Y. (1981). *A Jar of Dreams*. New York, NY: Macmillan.

Uchida, Y. (1992). *A Journey Home*. New York, NY: Macmillan.

Bibliography: Immigration

Anderson, M. (1989). *Searching for Shona*. New York, NY: Knopf.

Ashworth, M. (1992). *Children of the Canadian Mosaic: A Brief History to 1950*. Toronto, ON: OISE Press.

Bilson, G. (1982). *Death Over Montreal*. Toronto, ON: Kids Can Press.

Bilson, G. (1984). *Hockeybat Harris*. Toronto, ON: Kids Can Press.

Bohmer, H., & Wilson, D. (1987). *Mother Scorpion Country*. Chicago, IL: Children's Press.

Bridgers, S.E. (1980). *All Together Now*. New York, NY: Bantam.

Carlsson, J. (1989). *Camel Bells*. Toronto, ON: Groundwood.

Clark, A.N. (1976). *Secret of the Andes*. New York, NY: Puffin.

Coerr, E. (1979). *Sadako and the Thousand Paper Cranes*. New York, NY: Dell.

Conrad, P. (1987). *Prairie Songs*. New York, NY: HarperCollins.

Cooper, S. (1989). *Dawn of Fear*. New York, NY: Macmillan.

Crane Wartski, M. (1981). *A Boat to Nowhere*. New York, NY: New American Library/Dutton.

DeJong, M. (1987). *The House of Sixty Fathers*. New York, NY: Harper & Row.

Frank, R. (1986). *No Hero for the Kaiser*. New York, NY: Lothrop, Lee & Shepard.

Fritz, J. (1982). *Homesick: My Own Story*. New York, NY: Dell.

Gerstein, M. (1987). *The Mountains of Tibet*. New York, NY: Harper & Row.

Gordon, S. (1989). *Waiting for the Rain*. New York, NY: Bantam Books.

Hautzig, E. (1987). *The Endless Steppe*. New York, NY: Harper Collins.

Heneghan, J. (1988). *Promises to Come*. Don Mills, ON: General.

Hewitt, M., & Mackay, C. (1981). *One Proud Summer*. Toronto, ON: Women's Press.

Holman, F. (1985). *The Wild Children*. New York, NY: Puffin.

Isadora, R. (1991). *At the Crossroads*. New York, NY: Greenwillow Books.

Kerr, J. (1987). *When Hitler Stole Pink Rabbit*. New York, NY: Dell.

Laird, E. (1992). *Kiss the Dust*. New York, NY: Dutton.

Little, J. (1977). *From Anna*. Markham, ON: Fitzhenry & Whiteside.

Lowry, L. (1990). *Number the Stars*. New York, NY: Dell.

Lunn, J. (1992). *The Root Cellar.* Toronto, ON: Penguin.

Lunn, J., & Moore, C. (1992). *The Story of Canada.* Toronto, ON: Lester Publishing.

MacLachlin, P. (1987). *Sarah, Plain and Tall.* New York, NY: HarperCollins.

Magorian, M. (1986). *Goodnight Mister Tom.* New York, NY: Harper Collins.

McDermott, G. (1974). *Arrow to the Sun: A Pueblo Indian Tale.* New York, NY: Viking

Naidoo, B. (1988). *Journey to Jo'burg.* New York, NY: Harper Collins.

O'Dell, S. (1989). *Black Star, Bright Dawn.* New York, NY: Fawcett Juniper.

Orgel, D. (1988). *The Devil in Vienna.* New York, NY: Puffin.

Paterson, K. (1989). *Park's Quest.* New York, NY: Puffin.

Reiff, T. (1989). *Boat People: The Vietnamese.* Belmont, CA: Feron/Janus/Quercus.

Reiff, T. (1989). *Nobody Knows: The Africans.* Belmont, CA: Feron/Janus/Quercus.

Reiff, T. (1989). *The Magic Paper: The Mexicans.* Belmont, CA: Feron/Janus/Quercus.

Rohmer, H., & Rea, J. (1988). *Atariba and Niguayona.* Chicago, IL: Children's Press.

Smucker, B. (1991). *Days of Terror.* Toronto, ON: Penguin.

Surat, M.M. (1989). *Angel Child, Dragon Child.* New York, NY: Scholastic.

Truss, J. (1988). *Red.* Toronto, ON: Groundwood.

Truss, J., & Chambers, J. (1990). *A Very Small Rebellion.* Don Mills, ON: General.

Turner, H.D. (1988). *Rebel Run.* Agincourt, ON: Gage.

Yagawa, S. (1981). *The Crane Wife.* New York, NY: Mulberry Books.

Yolen, J. (1990). *The Devil's Arithmetic.* New York, NY: Puffin.

Bibliography: Social and Racial Justice

Carlsson, J. (1989). *Camel Bells.* Toronto, ON: Groundwood.

Coerr, E. (1979). *Sadako and The Thousand Paper Cranes.* New York, NY: Dell.

Doyle, B. (1982). *Angel Square.* Toronto, ON: Groundwood.

Fisher Staples, S. (1989). *Shabanu: Daughter of the Wind.* New York, NY: Knopf.

Gordon, S. (1989). *Waiting for the Rain.* New York, NY: Bantam.

Guy, R. (1992). *Edith Jackson.* New York, NY: Dell.

Hautzig, E. (1987). *The Endless Steppe.* New York, NY: Harper Collins.

Hewitt, M., & Mackay, C. (1981). *One Proud Summer.* Toronto, ON: Women's Press.

Kerr, J. (1977). *When Hitler Stole Pink Rabbit.* New York, NY: Dell.

Laird, E. (1992). *Kiss the Dust.* New York, NY: Dutton.

Lester, J. (1986). *To Be a Slave.* New York, NY: Scholastic.

Lowry, L. (1990). *Number the Stars.* New York, NY: Dell.

Lunn, J. (1992). *The Root Cellar.* Toronto, ON: Penguin.

Masters, A. (Ed.) (1989). *Taking Root: Canada from 1700 to 1760.* Ottawa, ON: Canada Communications.

Naidoo, B. (1988). *Journey to Jo'Burg.* New York, NY: Harper Collins.

Orgel, D. (1988). *The Devil in Vienna.* New York, NY: Puffin.

Paterson, K. (1989). *Park's Quest.* New York, NY: Puffin.

Paterson, K. (1992). *Lyddie.* New York, NY: Puffin.

Richter, H.P. (1987). *Friedrich.* New York, NY: Puffin.

Richter, H.P. (1987). *I Was There.* New York, NY: Puffin.

Strachan, I. (1992). *Journey of 1000 Miles.* Walter-on-Thames, UK: Nelson.

Taylor, M.D. (1991). *Let the Circle Be Unbroken.* New York, NY: Puffin.

Watson, J. (1992). *No Surrender.* London, UK: Lion Tracks.

Yolen, J. (1990). *The Devil's Arithmetic.* New York, NY: Puffin.

Young, H. (1980). *What Difference Does It Make Danny?* London, UK: Deutsch.

Index

Seurat, Maria M., 75
Short, Kathy, 28
Short stories, 24, 40, 45
Slides, 76
Social and racial justice, 33; as a core-study unit, 77-80
Steinbeck, John, 28, 29
Students: and learning abilities and styles, 11, 25, 28, 33, 45, 48; and cultural and linguistic backgrounds, 11-13; and levels of language proficiency, 11-13; and self-esteem and needs, 12-13; and preparation for the future, 14-15; and ownership of learning, 14-16, 18, 19, 20, 22, 35, 57; and theme studies, 20-22, 23-24; and elements of theme work, 24-27; and response activities, 28-32; and assessment and evaluation, 32; and a science-fiction focused-study unit, 35-44; and an ecology core-study unit, 45-56; and accessing prior knowledge and making predictions, 53-54; and a hazardous wastes core-study unit, 58-63; and a survival focused-study unit, 63-69; and an immigration focused-study unit, 71-77; and a social and racial justice core-study unit, 77-80
Surveys, 60, 61
Survival, as a focused-study unit, 63-69
Swiss Family Robinson, 66

Teacher-librarians, 36, 45, 46, 47, 63, 66, 73, 74, 76
Teachers: and meeting needs' of students, 11-13; and preparing students for the future, 14-15; and establishing learning environments, 15-17, 22; and working conditions, 17-18; and instituting themes, 20-22; and delivering content, 23; and choosing themes, 23-24; and elements of theme work, 24-27; and response activities, 28-32;

and theme formats, 32-33; and theme direction, 33; and theme order, 34; and a science fiction focused-study unit, 35-44; and an ecology core-study unit, 45-56; and common themes, 57-58; and a hazardous wastes core-study unit, 58-63; and a survival focused-study unit, 63-69; and frustrations experienced with theme work, 70-71; and an immigration focused-study unit, 71-77; and a social and racial justice core-study unit, 77-80
Television, 77
Tests, 23, 42, 44
Textbooks, 22, 23, 33, 45
Themes, 12-13, 19, 20-21; and success for all students, 22; choice of, 23-24, structure of, 24; elements of, 24-27; and response activities, 28-32; formats of, and sample topics, 32-33; direction of, 33; and ordering, 34; and a science fiction focused-study unit, 35-44; and an ecology core-study unit, 45-56; and common themes, 57-58; and a hazardous wastes core-study unit, 58-63; and a survival focused-study unit, 63-69; and potential frustrations, 70-71; and an immigration focused-study unit, 71-77; and a social and racial justice core-study unit, 77-80
Timelines, 25, 34, 74, 76
Timetables, 18, 21-22, 26, 27, 36, 57-58, 58-59, 63, 70, 73
Trust, between students and teachers, 15, 17, 18, 19; and themes, 21-22, 70-71
Turnbill, Ann, 64
Tutoring, 12

Verne, Jules, 38
Videos, 32, 41, 48, 61, 66, 67, 68, 77

Writers' workshops, 27

95